Christmas '92.

To:- Mary

With Best Wishes for Christmas

From:- Theresa & Paul xxx
                            xx

COLOUR IN LACE

When daisies pied and violets blue
And lady-smocks all silver-white
And cuckoo-buds of yellow hue
Do paint the meadows with delight

Love's Labours Lost
William Shakespeare

Fig. 1 *Harvest festival fan; coloured needlelace in cotton, silk and rayon threads, with the grey church (Honiton), grey ground (Bucks) and the sheaves (Bedfordshire) in bobbin lace*

COLOUR
IN LACE

Ann Collier

B.T. BATSFORD LIMITED · LONDON

© Ann Collier 1990

First published 1990

ISBN 0 7134 6394 5

Typeset by Servis Filmsetting Ltd, Manchester
and printed in Hong Kong
for the Publisher
B.T. Batsford Ltd
4 Fitzhardinge Street
London W1H 0AH

Contents

1. The principles of colour

The use of colour in any art form seems to create a problem for many of us, but colour is a natural occurrence and human eyes are equipped to interpret it. We do not know if everyone's perception of a given colour is the same; one person's red may be different from another's. The eye can discern a multitude of variations of a colour but the basic vocabulary assigned to them is very limited – blue, light blue, dark blue, etc. More sophisticated colour language likens colours to natural objects – kingfisher blue, peacock blue, turquoise blue, etc. – in order to define them more accurately.

Colours can cheer, depress, stimulate, tranquillize, provoke or antagonize, and we associate certain colours with emotional happenings in life – what excites one person will be hated by another. There is no doubt, however, that colours enrich our environment. We all have favourite colour schemes and it is a big step to venture into the unknown and try something different. This is even more apparent in lacemaking where the usual colours are white, ecru or black.

New colours are discovered from time to time, or rather existing colours acquire new names, and some colour combinations go in and out of fashion, e.g. navy with lime green or shocking pink with yellow. The Art Nouveau period gave us delicate pastel colours but a few years later, with Art Déco, these gave way to vibrant clashes of colour.

Animals and insects use colours as flight paths to flower nectar, as courtship display, as a danger signal or as camouflage; only man uses colour artistically in interior décor and dress decoration as well as for artistic expression. Many people are reluctant to exploit colour, perplexed by what clashes, matches or blends. We see colour all around us but find it difficult to use it, especially those of us with little or no art training. However, a colour sense arises naturally from observation of the world around us, although it can be developed further with training. It is difficult to be governed by a set of rules, but many artists and scientists have tried to formulate them and they can help the nervous. An early analysis by classical scholars related colours to the elements – earth, air, fire and water – and stated that colours were formed by blends of light. Centuries later Leonardo da Vinci proposed a similar theory – white light, yellow earth, green water, blue air, red fire and black darkness.

It took a scientist, Isaac Newton, to discover that ordinary sunlight comprises the colours of the rainbow – red, orange, yellow, green, blue, indigo and violet. He plotted them in a segmented circle to make the first colour wheel. Other theorists followed his ideas and there were many variations but it was this colour arrangement that was taught in the painting schools of Europe.

The commonest colour wheel takes red, yellow and blue in three equidistant segments of a circle and mixtures of red/yellow, blue/yellow and red/blue change gradually round the wheel with 'hot' colours (red, orange and purple) on one side and 'cool' colours (yellow, green and blue) on the other. The hot colours are favoured by many artists because of their dynamic and intense quality while cool colours create a sense of serenity and peace.

One of the great names in the history of colour is Michel Eugène Chevreul 1786–1889. He was a chemist and director of the dye house at the Gobelin tapestry works outside Paris, and was involved with the use of colour in tapestry weaving. He wrote the book *The Principles of Harmony and the Contrast of Colours*. Using the

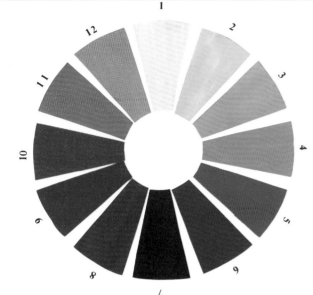

Fig. 2 *The colour wheel*

colour wheel (Fig. 2), he set out a series of principles and guide lines for colour harmony, which inspired many of the Impressionist painters.

Harmony

Perfect colour harmony occurs when adjacent colours on the colour wheel are used together. This harmony can be found in nature, such as the autumnal tints of orange, yellow, gold, red and brown. A red rose will contain orange highlights and purple shadows; nasturtiums are in the yellow-to-red range with yellow/green leaves.

Opposites or complementary colours

Colour combinations that are diametrically opposite to one another on the wheel are also very common in nature, e.g. violets with bright–yellow centres, an azure–blue sky with an orange/red sunset, red holly-berries on a dark-green bush and there are many more. Use **1** with **7**, **2** with **8**, etc.

Split complements

Split complements are used to create a more subtle colour scheme, by taking a colour and combining it with the colours on either side of its opposite – such as red with yellow/green and blue/green, **9** with **2** and **4**, **1** with **8** and **6**, **3** with **8** and **10**, etc.

Triads

These are the colours that form an equilateral triangle within the circle:

red–yellow–blue (9–1–5) are the primary colours and form a strong combination,

orange–green–violet (11–3–7) give a more refined combination,

red/orange–yellow/green–blue/violet (10–2–6) give a startling appearance,

yellow/orange–blue/green–red/violet (12–4–8) is a combination much favoured by Oriental artists.

Dominant colours

This technique makes use of one dominant colour mixed with other colours to form an harmonious whole. This is often seen in nature such as when a view is washed with a yellow glow in evening sunshine, or enveloped in a purple/grey mist. Artists noted these effects and used them, e.g. the golden glow seen in many Titian paintings. This method of blending colour can be very attractive and used to good effect when blending threads.

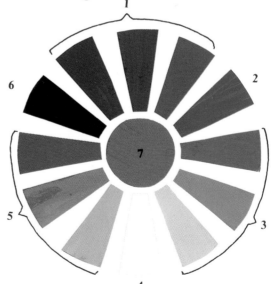

Fig. 3 *Tint–Shade–Colour wheel: 1-shades, 2-colour, 3-tints, 4-white, 5-grey, 6-black and 7-tone*

The simplest colour scheme is created using a limited palette, consisting of one colour in different shades and tints. A colour mixed with black is a shade, mixed with white is a tint, and black, white and any colour mixed in equal quantities form a tone. These can be mixed in paint to get the general idea and then threads found to correspond; manufacturers usually produce a range of such coloured threads numbered consecutively.

The shade–tint–tone–colour circle will harmonize in any combination chosen. The Impressionist painters used colour–tint–white for a luminous effect, Rembrandt used colour–shade–black to create deeper hues.

Experimenting in tones, shades and tints is an interesting exercise and produces some unexpected results; for instance, yellow mixed with black produces an olive-green tinge, yet no blue has been added. However, the best way to learn about colour is everyday observation: arranging flowers, choosing seeds from a catalogue, arranging fruit, even cooking and serving a meal.

The first steps into the world of colour can be based on natural things and thus we can test the colour theory. Take any flower, leaf, vegetable, piece of stone, etc. and see how many colours you can find in it. Now find threads to match these – mixtures of any kind – dull, shiny, textured, etc. It is amazing to find just how harmonious nature's palette is and how many colours there are in the commonest things. Take, for example, a turnip; it has large amounts of cream and small amounts of mauve, green, rust and orange. Note the colour proportions, because nature is never wrong.

Some optical illusions

● When dark and light colours are used side by side, the dark appear darker and the light lighter.
● A dull colour alongside a bright colour has the same effect – the dull becomes drab and the bright colour more vivid.
● Bright colours appear larger than dark colours and yellow appears the largest.
● Tints appear larger than shades.
● Red, in small quantities, livens up a colour scheme; blue/green will quieten it down.

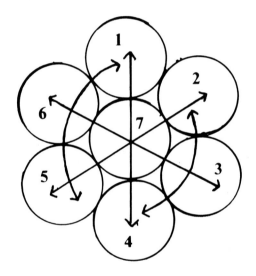

Diag. 1 *Colour/tint/shade. Any combination will work as shown by arrows. 1-colour, 2-tint, 3-white, 4-grey, 5-black, 6-shade, 7-tone*

2. Lace techniques in colour

Lace, by definition, is a textile of open construction which does not need a backing. There are many ways of making this open-work textile and most of these – crochet, macramé, tatting, Teneriffe and knitting – have been made in colour for many years.

Traditionally, bobbin, needle- and Carrickmacross laces have always been made in white, ecru or occasionally black. Coloured bobbin lace has been apparent in the peasant laces of Europe for centuries, used to blend and enhance the highly coloured traditional costumes, and the modern lace artists of eastern Europe had no hesitation in continuing with the colour tradition in the twentieth century. The areas with a strong tradition of fine thread laces – Bucks., Beds., Honiton, Mechlin, Chantilly, Brussels, Alençon, etc., have never produced coloured lace in any significant quantity. It was tried, but was not popular, and as it was a commercial industry sales were all-important, and fashion had to be catered for. A few experiments have been tried in recent years, and colour in bobbin lace is gaining in popularity, although it is difficult to control the threads in continuous one-piece bobbin lace.

The strong tradition of needlelace on the Continent, in areas such as Alençon and Brussels, has had little room for colour experimentation because it has been all-important to keep the white lace tradition alive; but, in England, needlelace has been worked in colour as well as in white; it was used for the stump work boxes of the seventeenth century. The coloured threads are much easier to control in needlelace than in bobbin lace.

The embroidered laces such as Carrickmackross, Limerick and Tambour were introduced in the mid-nineteenth century to encourage a lace industry using imported machine-made net. The intention was to copy the ninetee-th-century bobbin and needlelaces and the fashionable colours were white, ecru or black.

Why put colour into lace at all? It is very beautiful in white because of the numerous stitches which provide texture, and the wrong technique or the wrong colour selection can destroy some of the beauty. This is why many people are not drawn to the use of colour and yet it is not generally considered that all embroidery should be in white – so why not make lace in colour? The correct choice of technique and colour scheme is all-important to make a piece of artistic merit. The use of colour does make lace-making more exciting and stimulating and the more one does, the more adventurous one becomes. Lace-making is time-consuming and one has to be prepared to experiment before a final decision can be made on technique, colour, design and choice of thread.

In the eighteenth and nineteenth centuries, when lace-making was in its heyday, there were very few fine, coloured threads but now there is an unlimited supply. We have variegated and textured ones, metallic and shiny ones, available in linen, wool, silk, cotton and rayon; the way to find out if they are suitable is to try them. The only completely unsuitable ones are those in nylon or Terylene (Dacron) as they are very elastic.

Fig. 4 *Clematis plant*

The intended use for the lace is the most important factor when choosing threads: has it to be laundered, and if so, how often? Is it ornamental? Does it have to match a décor? If there is an order of procedure, the problems can be solved systematically:

1. The purpose of the piece.
2. The design.
3. The technique to be used.
4. The size of the piece.
5. The colour scheme.
6. The sort of thread.
7. The size of thread.

General note re materials

The DMC Broder Machine range has replaced both Retors d'Alsace *and* Brillante d'Alsace.

Where 50 Linen is required, please use Bockens (Swedish) thread or ask your supplier for an equivalent weight.

The following designs have been taken from a clematis plant and by adapting them for bobbin, needle- and Carrickmacross lace they show the variations that are possible within the different techniques. The colours are dark and light green, cream and pink.

Diag. 2 *Needlelace flower*

NEEDLELACE MOTIF

For dress-appliqué, pendant, mobile or box top.

Materials required

Threads in green, pink and cream: 100/3 silk, 50 cotton or rayon; soft tacking cotton that breaks easily; a fine needle; a ball point needle; architect's linen or tracing paper and plastic film; a piece of firm cotton material.

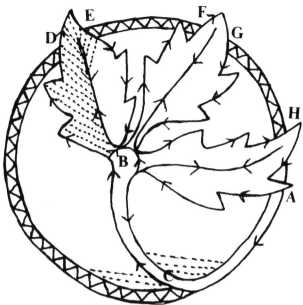

Diag. 3 *Needlelace leaves for box top*

Fig. 5 *Box lid worked in needlelace from a clematis design*

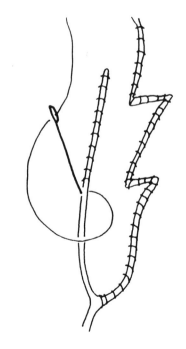

Diag. 4 *Couching the outline thread*

Method

Trace the design (*Diag. 3*) on to architect's linen or tracing paper covered with plastic adhesive film.

Prick every line with a fine needle at 2mm ($\frac{1}{16}$in) intervals.

Tack the pattern to a double piece of firm cotton material.

Start at **A**. Take a double thread of green, long enough to go round all the leaves in one continuous piece and couch it down with the tacking thread through the paper and material. Bring the needle up and down through the same pre-pricked hole. This outlining thread forms the firm base on which all the filling stitches are worked. Use a knot in the tacking thread to begin, and end with a few back stitches on the reverse of the work. These will be removed when the work is finished. If part of the design has a dead end and cannot be worked continuously (e.g. leaf veins) couch a single thread up and back, thus forming a double. The continuous route of this outlining thread is important to all needlelace, and always needs careful planning.

Finish at **A** and whip the threads to the existing leaf outline.

Join a new double green thread to make the circular frame by looping it through the existing couched outline at **C**. Couch from **C** to **D** and **D** to **C**, use the same threads to make whipped bars between the lines as in *Diag. 5*. Work **E** to **F** and **G** to **H** in the same way.

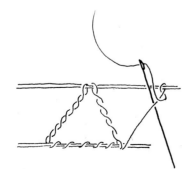

Diag. 5 *Whipped bars*

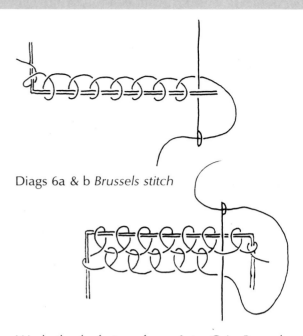

Diags 6a & b *Brussels stitch*

Work the leaf stem from **A** to **C** in Brussels stitch, as in *Diags 6a & b*, beginning and ending the thread by whipping over the couched outline. Always make sure that there is enough thread to finish the line; do not start or finish in the middle of a row.

Work corded Brussels stitch as in *Diag. 7*, in the leaves working in the direction indicated by the dotted lines. Work the first row into the outline from edge to vein and subsequent rows in the loops of the previous row, taking the thread under and over the couching at the leaf edge and the central vein.

Work pea stitch (*Diag. 9*) in dark green in the background areas in the direction indicated by the dotted lines.

Work the final top-stitched edge by laying four threads on the existing outline and following the original route. Buttonhole stitch closely with the knotted edge to the outside, over these threads and the outlining thread. As with the couching, when a vein is reached, take two threads up and back to keep the continuity.

Take out the tacking threads that hold the pattern to the material and separate the two pieces of cotton material. The couching threads should break but if not they can be cut with scissors. Carefully lift the lace from the pattern and remove the ends of tacking cotton.

The Flowers

These are worked in cream and pink by the same method. Outline in a double cream thread and work corded Brussels stitch in the direction indicated by the dotted lines. The centre vein is a row of holes as in *Diag. 8*. Work a buttonhole ring (couronne) as in *Diag. 10* and attach to the flower centre. Work bullion knots or sew on beads to make the stamens. Attach to the leaves.

This is the working method for all the needle-lace in this book and because of the use of colour it has been slightly adapted from the traditional method used when working in white.

The outlining thread is the same one as is used for the fillings, so that at the end of the couching the thread can be used to start the stitching, so ensuring that it is well attached. This is particularly useful when working small areas of different colours since the outline can be made in small pieces. If the couching thread is a tacking cotton or Honiton thread that breaks easily, the separation of the double material at the end is easier.

Brussels stitch

Introduce a thread by whipping a few stitches to the outlining and, with the needle away from you, work an even row of buttonhole stitches through the couched threads so that the stitches lie on the surface.

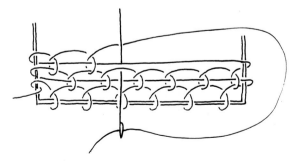

Diag. 7 *Corded Brussels stitch*

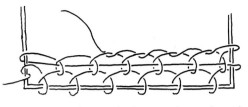

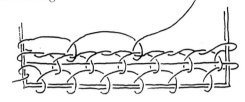

Diags 8a & b *Corded Brussels stitch with holes to form veining*

At the end of the row (*Diag. 6b*), take the thread under and over the couched threads and turn the work. Work the next row of stitches from left to right with the needle towards you into each loop of the previous row. Continue until the space is filled, then whip the filling to the upper couched threads.

Corded Brussels stitch

Work each row from left to right with the needle away from you.

Work the first row as for Brussels stitch and at the right-hand side, take the thread under and over the edge and bring it straight back to the left-hand side (*Diag. 7*). Take it under and over the outline and repeat row one including the laid thread.

Corded Brussels stitch with holes

Work corded Brussels stitch until the holes are required, whip the thread back through each loop of the previous row from right to left, instead of bringing it straight back (*Diag. 8a*).

Work the next row by working alternate stitches (*Diag. 8b*), whip back to the left-hand side again and work two stitches in the large loop. Continue in corded Brussels stitch.

Working two or three rows of corded and one row of holes repeatedly, creates another filling.

Pea stitch

Work the first row as in Brussels stitch from left to right with the needle away from you. Turn, and with the needle towards you, work two stitches, miss two stitches. Turn and work three stitches in the large loop and one stitch in the small loop (*Diag. 9*).

Repeat the second row making sure that the two worked stitches come in the centre of the previous large loop and the two missed stitches are over the small loop.

Couronnes or buttonhole rings

Wind the thread six to eight times round a knitting needle of appropriate size or a ring stick, and use the thread-end to buttonhole stitch round the ring (*Diag. 10*). This can be done with the threads still on the ring or held in the hand. Alternatively, the threads can be whipped to an existing outlined ring on the pattern and buttonholed *in situ*.

BOBBIN LACE

There is a subtle difference between colour in lace and coloured lace, especially in bobbin lace techniques. A piece of lace can be made in a colour to match décor or dress but to add colour into white lace in small areas requires

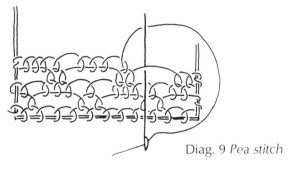

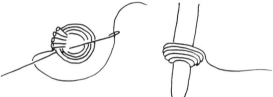

Diag. 9 *Pea stitch*

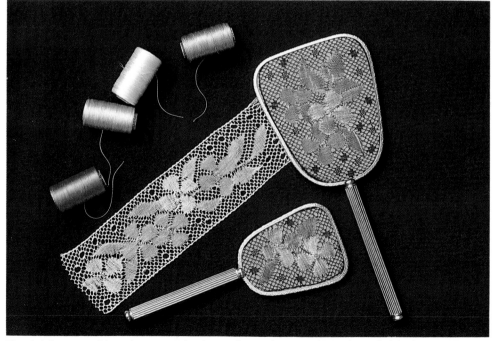

Diag. 10 *Couronnes*

Fig. 6 *Mirror and brush set worked in coloured rayon threads with black passives, the panel is in the same threads but with white passives*

quite a different techinque. The Honiton technique, whereby small cloth- or half-stitch areas are worked and then joined with sewings, is the easiest way to control several colours, and most of the designs in my previous books have been made in this way.

Adding colour to a multi-thread lace such as Torchon, Bedfordshire or Bucks, is more difficult. The passive threads which can be accommodated in the lace weaving process also have to make the open ground stitches and the colour is hard to control. Many of the rules for a one-colour lace have to be modified and the design and movement of the colours must be carefully worked out beforehand. Before embarking on colour in lace, basic lace-making techniques must be mastered so that there is an understanding of the thread movements; a grounding in Torchon forms a good basis for this type of free lace.

The weaving technique, the integral part of bobbin lace, allows the coloured threads to intermingle. To control the colour use it only as the weaving thread and keep the passive threads in cream, white or black.

The solid areas of the design have to be worked in cloth stitch and the use of fancy fillings confined to the background. As can be seen in *Fig. 6*, shades and tints can be achieved by using white, cream or black passives although much of the shading within the design occurs by accident. The passives can become closer or wider spaced during working to create different effects. In *Fig. 6* the same coloured threads have been used in both the strip and the mirror set; only the passives are different. Black always gives a dramatic effect. It is important to use a bright thread because it is always toned down by the passives and in some cases a shiny thread can be used to contrast with the duller background threads. The coloured weavers will always dominate and can be carried through or over the pattern or alternatively tied and cut off at the end of a piece. Work is always carried out on the wrong side of the piece.

Diag. 11 *Clematis strip (colour coded)*

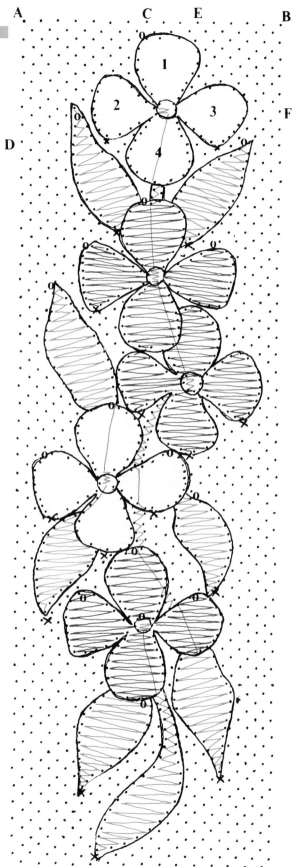

15

Clematis spray

This can be used for a door finger-plate, picture, or as an insert in a garment, cloth, place-mat or lampshade. It can form a repeat pattern.

There is no gimp, the black outline is for use in Carrickmacross.

Suitable threads

For the passives – 50 linen or DMC Broder Machine 50 (32 prs), and for the weavers – DMC Broder Machine 50 or a comparable rayon thread (7 prs green, 6 prs red, 6 prs orange).

Method

Hang 2 prs white on each pinhole from **A** to **B** and work Torchon ground from **C** to **D** and **E** to **F**. Begin the top petal by adding 1 pr orange at **0** and cloth stitch to the centre leaving pairs out for petals **2** and **3**. Add 1 pr green at the centre to make a tally with another pair of white.

Begin petals **2** and **3** with 1 pr orange on either side. Cloth stitch, taking in the pairs from petal **1** and the ground, and dropping pairs out for the leaves and petal **4**.

Tie and cut off the coloured weavers at **X** but carry the orange pair from petal **1** through petal **4**. Make a tally with 1 pr white and 1 pr green using the green as the weaver. Anchor the ends by tying and take the threads into petal **4** but remove the green pair after the first row and leave them to one side.

Complete petal **4** and bring in the green pair again at the base to weave the stalk. Use the orange pair as passives in the next flower. Join in the green pair, carrying the thread over the back of petal **4**, and make the stalk, incorporating the spare orange pair.

Cloth stitch the leaves by adding green pairs at **0** and work down to the first red petal, attach the green stalk pair but leave it to one side.

Start the red flower with a red pair and work petal and leaves simultaneously, meeting the weavers. Tie off the green pairs at **X**. Join in a green pair at the centre and make a tally in green as before.

Start the other two petals with red pairs at **0**; cut off one of these at **X**, leaving the other for the third flower.

Proceed in the same way down the panel adding pairs at **0** and taking them out at **X**. Carry green pairs over the back where convenient. Finish the panel by tying off the pairs at the base and weaving them back or, in the case of a repeat pattern used on a lampshade, join to itself.

Brush and Mirror Set

These show the difference in appearance when using black passives with the same coloured weavers as in the small panel.

Mirror back

37 prs black, 3 prs green, 2 prs orange, 4 prs red.

Diag. 12 *Brush back*

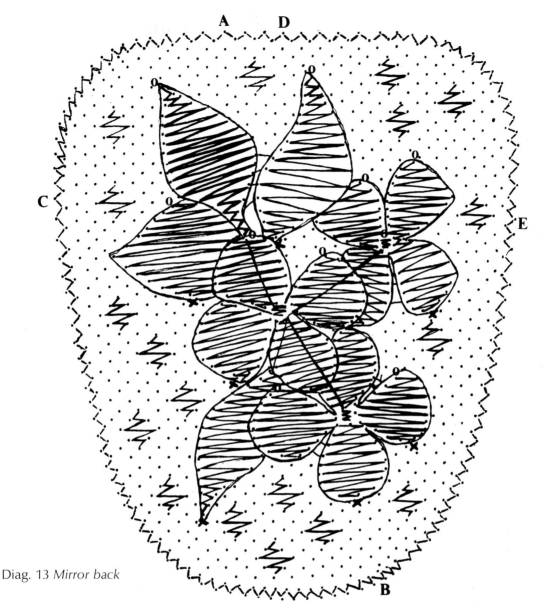

Diag. 13 *Mirror back*

Method

Lay 2 prs of passives across the top and, starting with 2 prs at **A**, make a narrow braid to left and right adding 2 prs at each pinhole on the inside of the braid. Continue on either side taking pairs in and out of it as required. Work the ground simultaneously.

Establish the Torchon ground from **A** to **C** and **D** to **E**. There are small cloth-stitch diamonds in this ground to give added interest.

Begin the leaves at **0** and work as for the small panel, carrying the threads over where possible, or cutting off at **X**. The weavers of the petals and leaves meet in several places and this gives a tidier finish.

At the base, take the passives into the small braid and remove them, ending at **B** where they meet.

Brush back

27 prs black, 2 prs green, 3 prs cream, 3 prs orange.

Work in the same way as the mirror back.

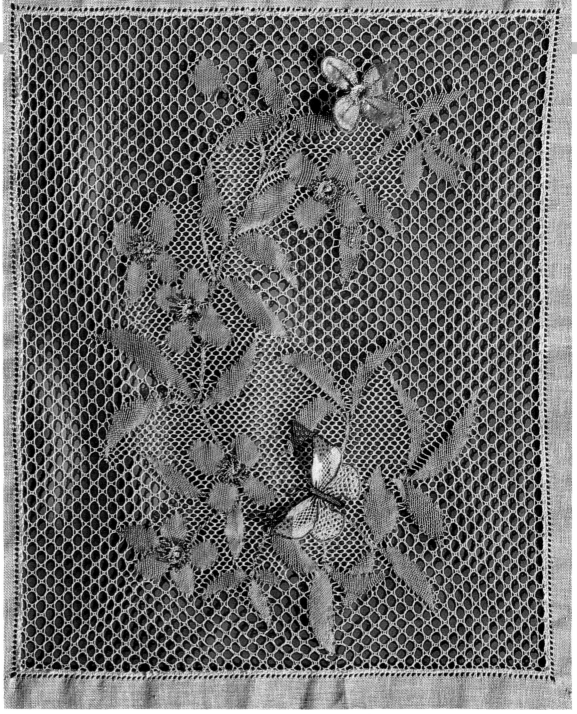

Fig. 7 *Large panel of clematis made as a fire screen. This differs slightly from* Diag. 14 *as it was experimental; two grounds were used and an extra dimensional flower was added*

Large spray
100 prs white, 16 prs red, 22 prs green.

This follows the same principle as for the small panel but being much larger it is more compli-cated. It is suitable for a picture in the size given, or it can be enlarged in which case the size of thread must be adjusted. It is advisable to try the small panel first if you have not worked in colour before.

Diag. 14 *Large clematis panel (colour coded)*

Diag. 15 *Large clematis panel (use with* Diag. 14)

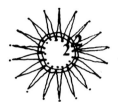

Diag. 16 *Fringed centre for flowers*

Method

Hang in 10 prs at **A** and use 5 of them to make the top braid (the other 5 prs are for the left-hand braid). Hang 2 prs at each pinhole on the inside of this braid to **B** — these are the ground pairs.

Establish **C** to **D**, and **E** to **F** before commencing the spray. The ground used is Honeycomb and this gives a pleasant contrast to the design.

Add coloured pairs at **0** and remove them at **X**. Many of the leaves and flowers are worked simultaneously, meeting the weavers.

Work green tallies as flower centres and carry over the green pair for the stalk. Green pairs gradually accumulate, adding to the general shading. They can be left in until the stalks become too cramped. The green weaving pairs may cross from stalk to flower centre to another stalk over the back of the work.

Work the ground continuously in blocks so that pairs are always ready for the next flower section.

Work fringed centres from *Diag. 16* separately with 2 prs of cream passives and a green weaver, and stitch them to the flowers on completion of main panel.

Pictures or hangings such as this can be framed by attaching threads to the lace sides and tying them at intervals through holes drilled in the frame; alternatively the lace can be sewn on to a piece of linen which is hem stitched, and this can be attached to the frame.

This design can also be worked in needlelace. Trace the flower spray omitting the net dots and work as in all needlelace. Some of the flowers may be worked separately to achieve a three-dimensional effect.

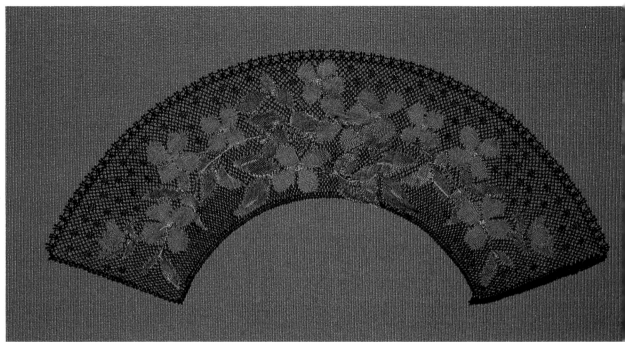

Fig. 8 *Clematis fan leaf worked with mauve and green rayon weavers and black passives*

Fig. 9 *Close up of the fan in* Fig. 8

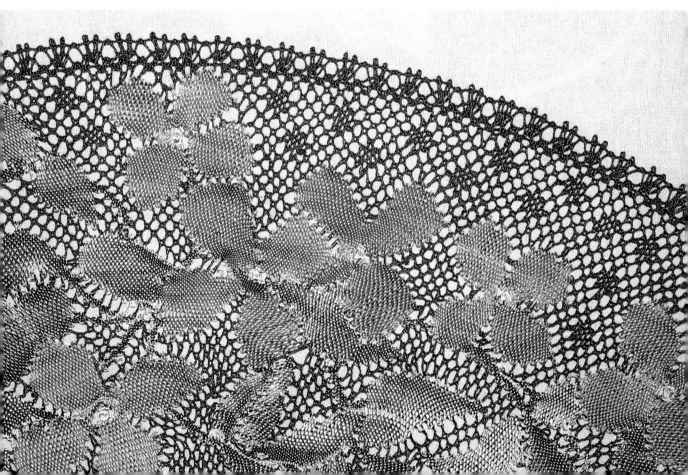

Fan or yoke

Interesting designs can be made in circles and half circles and there are several examples in this book. A design can be within a circle as in the following pattern, needing the addition of an edge, or the edge can be part of the design as in *Diag. 19* and *Fig. 13*. Half circles can be used as fan leaves or dress yokes (inset into the garment) or worn as loose front collars. A complete circle can be used on a cushion or as a full collar.

Diag. 17a *Clematis fan (colour coded)*

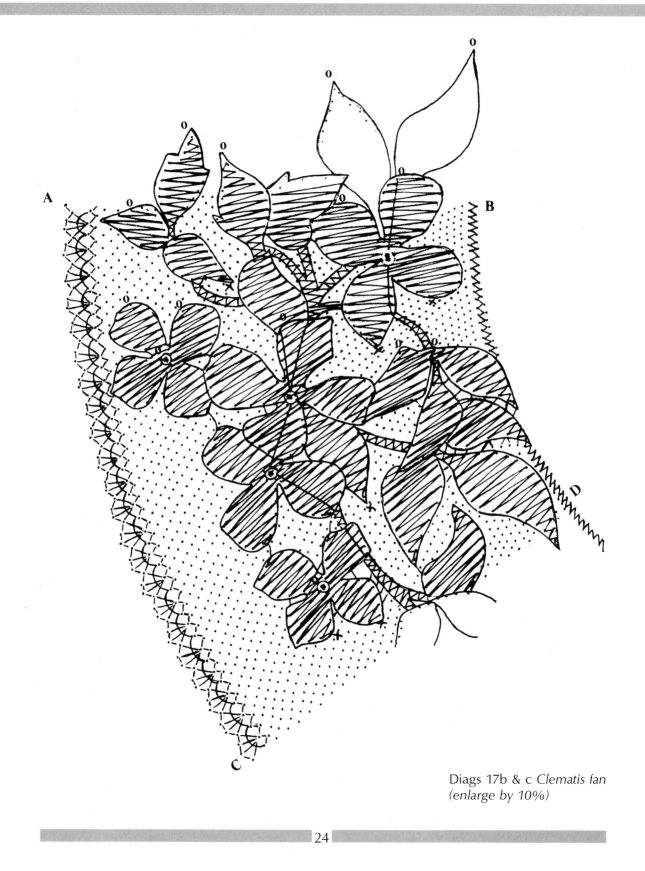

Diags 17b & c *Clematis fan*
(enlarge by 10%)

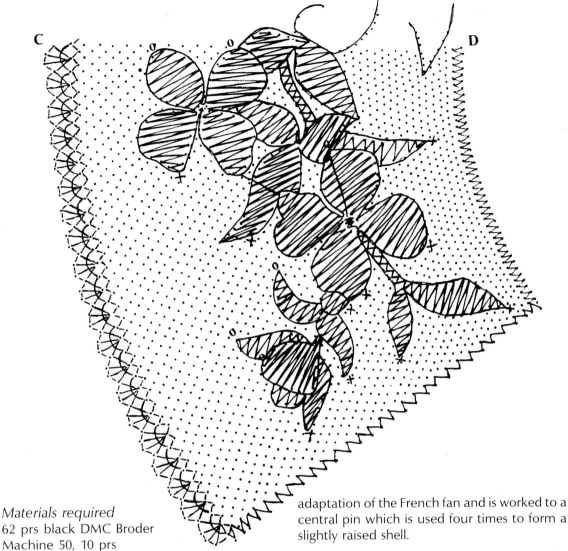

Materials required

62 prs black DMC Broder Machine 50, 10 prs purple, 10 prs green (approx.).

Method

Try the small panel first if you have not worked in colour before.

Join pattern pieces **AB** to **AB** and **CD** to **CD** and work as for the small panel (described on *p. 15*) adding coloured pairs at **0** and carrying them through wherever possible or cutting them off at **X**. Begin the shell edge at **E**.

Make a small braid from **E** to **F**, hanging 2 prs from it on every pinhole. The edge is an adaptation of the French fan and is worked to a central pin which is used four times to form a slightly raised shell.

Establish the ground from **G** to **H** and follow the diagram. The ground has been plotted on circular graph paper and the lines will form arcs rather than straight lines.

The circular movement of the ground allows gradual movement of the pillow, to change the direction without distorting the ground.

The yoke from *Diag. 17* is shown in *Fig. 12* worked in Carrickmacross and following the instructions.

Most bobbin lace designs in this chapter can be worked in needlelace or Carrickmacross, using the black outlines on the patterns.

Fig. 10 *Clematis panels in Carrickmacross, embroidered and painted*

Needlelace

Trace off the main flower shapes without the net markings and work as instructed for needlelace. The flower can be mounted on material or net.

Carrickmacross

Carrikmacross is a form of appliqué on fine lawn net or organdie. It is important that the applied material is transparent enough to display the quality of the lace, and the method is the same as for traditional white work. The colour is added at the end. It is possible to apply different coloured materials but the effect is very different.

There are three ways to achieve colour:
1. Painting with fabric paints.
2. Using fabric crayons.
3. Darning the net at the back of the applied pieces.

Fig. 11 *Close up of the darning stitch on the clematis panel on the wrong side*

Fig. 12 *Blouse yoke in Carrickmacross worked from* Diag. 17 *and darned in shades of blue and green. The edge is worked as in* Diag. 18c

No. 3 gives a satisfactory result similar to that of shadow embroidery. Strong, bright colours are necessary as they will be very subdued by the organdie overlay and give a soft pastel effect on the right side.

The design is again taken from the clematis and made into a long spray to form a repeat pattern. It can be used under a finger-plate, inserted into a blouse, or as an edging for a lampshade. Carrickmacross can be made as an integral part of the finished piece; a napkin in lawn can have just the corner worked, a blouse can have insets so that there is no need to apply the lace.

Materials required

Cotton organdie or cotton lawn, cotton net, perle 12 or coton à broder 40 in white, one thread of stranded cotton for couching, architect's linen or tracing paper covered with plastic film, sharp scissors – there are special ones for Carrickmacross work with one pointed blade and the other rounded.

Method

Pre-wash the net and organdie to soften and shrink them.

Trace the pattern outline from the bobbin

clematis designs in *Diags 11, 12, 13* or *Diags 14, 15, or 17* on to architect's linen or tracing paper covered with plastic film.

Place the net on top of the design and cover the net with the organdie.

Tack the three layers firmly together, tacking between the pattern lines as well, so that the whole piece is firm.

Take enough thicker thread to go all round the design in a continuous line and, starting at the top, couch this thread with the thin one. Form stitches 1mm ($\frac{1}{32}$in) apart, working only through the net and the organdie, *not* through the pattern. When there is a dead-end or where the flower petals indent, couch the thread up and back. Start and finish the couching threads by backstitching.

Finish by doubling the thread where it meets for 1cm ($\frac{3}{8}$in).

Remove all the tacking threads and lift the lace from the pattern.

Cut away the organdie from the background of the design, leaving the net exposed. Take great care, as one careless snip will ruin the work. In confined spaces such as flower centres lift the organdie between the fingers and make a small snip first.

Darn the net at the back of the design with two threads of coloured stranded cotton as in *Diag. 18a*. Make sure that you keep within the edge and that the thread does not go through the organdie. A strong colour can be chosen because it will be toned down by the organdie. Various shades of pink are suitable for the flowers and shades of green for the leaves.

Work a buttonholed ring in the centre of the flowers, allowing the stitches to overlay the petals and pull tight enough to make a hole in the net.

Finally, work stem stitch for the veins.

The Yoke pattern shown in *Fig. 12* can be made into a complete circle to use as a small cloth or a collar. Work the edge as in *Diag. 18c*.

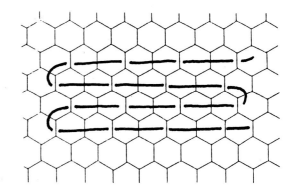

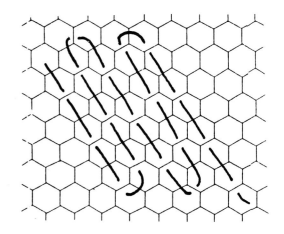

Diags 18a & b *Darning on net*

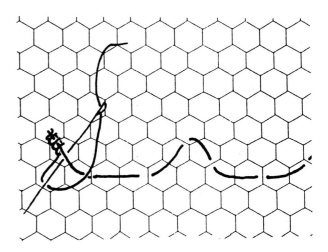

Diag. 18c *Finishing a net edge*

Diag. 19 *Roses and butterflies for Carrickmacross or needlelace*

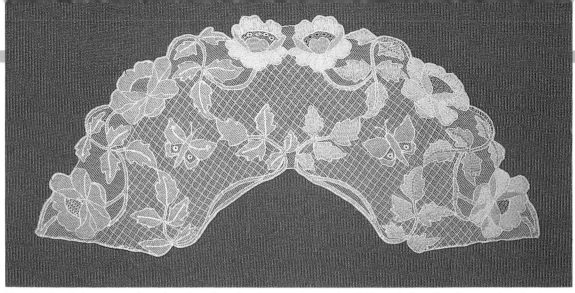

Fig. 13 *Carrickmacross fan showing the darning partly worked; the left-hand side is unfinished*

Roses and butterflies

The roses motif has been taken from an antique piece of needlelace and adapted for Carrickmacross.

The pattern is a repeat when reversed and will make a half circle for a dress yoke or fan; a complete circle will make a small table centre.

Method

Trace the pattern appropriately for the desired use and work the Carrickmacross as explained previously. Work firm, loop stitch on the outer edge or make picots as in *Diag. 20*.

Cut away the net and organdie to this edge and also cut away the organdie from around the design marked **X**.

Work buttonhole rings for the spots on the butterfly and darn the net at the back of the organdie.

Diag. 20 *Carrickmacross picots*

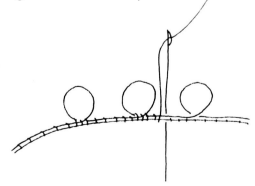

Shading can be achieved by darning with a darker thread on the upturned petals. The darning can be worked in any direction of the net mesh and textural patterns can be achieved with careful arrangement and direction of working.

Work stem stitch on the surfaces of petals and leaves and work fillings from *Diag. 21* in the flower centres.

Motifs can be taken from this design for use on small items such as trinket-box lids or paper-weights. The butterfly is particularly useful.

Needlelace

This design can be made in needlelace. *Fig. 14* shows the stitches to use and the instructions are on *pp. 10–13*. Parts of it can be used for appliqué on dress and the outer edge can be used as a collar.

CARRICKMACROSS FILLINGS

There are hundreds of variations of darning on net that can produce a wealth of attractive filling stitches, all suitable for filling in the cut-out areas of Carrickmacross.

To make a neat edge

Darn a thick thread in a curved shape and buttonhole stitch over it as shown in *Diag. 18*. The edge can also be worked straight or serrated, the path of the thick thread gives the outline.

Stitches

Patterned stitches on net are worked with a fine, soft thread – one thread of stranded cotton is suitable. Follow the diagrams.

Fig. 14 *Carrickmacross and needlelace motif from* Diag. 23

Diag. 21 *Carrickmacross filling stitches*

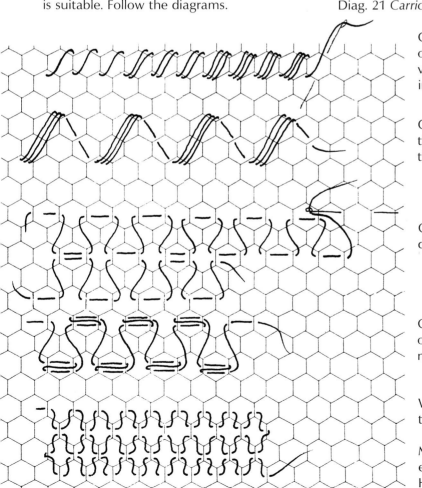

Oversew each hexagonal hole once, twice or three times – variations of density are produced in this way.

Oversew three or four times – this is suitable for larger areas as the stitches are widely spaced.

Cobweb stitch – produces a delicate all-over pattern.

Cobweb stitch variation – oversew three times before moving to the row below.

Wave stitch – slanted weaving that produces a flat area of colour.

More can be devised using embroidery stitches such as Herringbone, Cross stitch, Fly stitch.

Diag. 22 *Flower motif for Carrickmacross or needlelace*

Diag. 23 *Rose motif for Carrickmacross or needlelace*

3. Colour and design from natural sources

A historical study of lace reveals that there has always been a separation between designer and worker. This is not so much the case today since many more people design their own pieces, but *colour* has always been a stumbling block for the craftsman.

The ability to draw and design is found in fewer people than the ability to master manual skills and most lace-makers have had to rely on someone else for their patterns. These patterns were made by skilled artists and the designs reflected the times that they lived in and contemporary fashion. Natural themes such as flowers, animals, insects and birds have always been popular, because they offer an unlimited fund of ideas. However, there is a difference between traditional and contemporary design and most lace-makers who design are some-where between the two. The use of colour is just another step in the modern direction.

Embroidery has gone through many phases to the present day, first copying the designs of the past, then a modern approach using very little stitchery, and now good design, with new interpretations of the best traditional stitches. Lace will probably go through similar phases, now that its revival is firmly established, but most people are aware now that a good knowledge of techniques is essential for good design. Lace today has a different use to the past; it is becoming accepted as another art form and colour is now being used.

There are certain principles of design which must be observed when using colour, and to do this it is most important that the design is 'painted up' using either paints or felt pens before the final colours are selected. Do not rely on what you *think* it will look like. The design principles to check are:

1. Proportion
This is the relationship between the various units that make up the design; colour can destroy or enhance this.

2. Focal point
This is the centre of interest to which the eye is immediately drawn and to which all other parts should be related. A dominant colour can be used effectively here but the eye must be encouraged to encompass the whole design. Without a focal point a design becomes a rambling pattern of shapes.

3. Balance
This can be observed everywhere in nature. Whether symmetrical or asymmetrical, the design should still retain balance: it should not be top or bottom heavy or one-sided.

4. Rhythm
This is the 'flow' of the design, the co-ordination, harmony and contrast, created by a mixture of straight and curved lines that give a feeling of movement.

In addition to these guidelines there is an instinctive use of line and colour. The ability to adapt what one sees into a design is invaluable and the choice of colour is then no problem. A good design should be capable of interpretation in any media with slight adjustment, and this is equally true of lace. The following designs have been worked out for specific techniques but many of them can be worked in other lace forms and this is indicated where applicable.

Fig. 15 *Bobbin lace parasol made in eight panels representing wild flowers throughout the year*

FLOWER PANELS IN BOBBIN LACE

The ground is Torchon, but with holes introduced to break the monotony. This technique is often employed by Eeva-Liisa Kortelahti (Finland).

The following four patterns are from a set of eight that were used to make the parasol in *Fig. 15*. They were worked as triangles so that they made a domed circle but they are given here as rectangles so that they can be used as pictures or insertions into lampshades or cushions. They are worked in the same way as the clematis sprays but using more colours.

Once the technique has been mastered it is possible to design other panels taking inspiration from seed catalogues, birthday cards, embroidery designs, flower books, etc. Different ground stitches may be used to give more background interest.

Briar Roses

Materials required

30 DMC Spécial Dentelles or comparable thread, 68 prs white (w), 6 prs pink (p), 24 prs green (g).

Add coloured pairs as indicted by the letters and remove them at **X**.

Method

Work on the wrong side. The black outline is not a gimp, it is to indicate the outline for Carrickmacross or needlelace.

Set up 2 prs on each pinhole from **A** to **B** through 2 prs of passives laid across the top. These form a firm edge for the top and sides. Establish **C** to **D** and **E** to **F** in Torchon ground with holes made as indicated in the pattern.

Start the bud at **p** and work down to the base leaving out pairs for the second pink petal and green leaf. Work the white outer petals at the same time and, at the base, take the pink pair (twisted) up to the top of the second petal, treating it as a gimp. Work the second petal and at the base take the pink pair up to the top of the third petal. Begin leaflets at **g** and work leaflets and bud base all in one.

Start the first rose flower by making the pink tip and first and second petals simultaneously, leaving pairs out for the petals on either side.

Add a green pair and make a tally in the flower centre; carry the pair over the worked bottom petal for the stem. Work the stem and stump followed by the first two rose leaves.

At the base of the leaf stalk add two green pairs and pass them through the ground as a gimp. Work the two lower rose leaves. Use these gimp pairs to work the fifth rose leaf in two parts; work the upper half of the leaf first, then the lower half meeting both weavers at the tip. Continue the stem and make the second set of rose leaves. Work the second flower in the same way as the first.

At this stage flowers, stems and leaves are being worked simultaneously. Carry the green pairs from the stems and flower centres over the worked petals wherever possible; they will accumulate in the stems and so add to the shading.

Add two green pairs to form the lower curved leaf stalks and work the leaves as before.

Finish threads off in the lower edge. Embroider clusters of French knots to make stamens on completion of bobbin lace.

To make in other lace forms trace off the main spray without the net dots following the black outline.

Carrickmacross

Follow the instructions in chapter 2 and shade the flower tips in a strong pink, leaving the flowers white. Shade the leaves green.

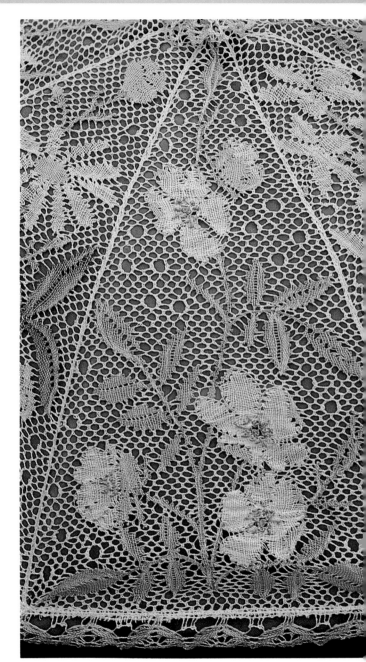

Fig. 16 *Briar roses representing June*

Needlelace

Use the rose spray in *Fig. 29* as a guide; work the flowers in pink and white as in chapter 2, and the leaves in two shades of green. The edges may be wired by adding thin fuse wire to the last top stitching to give a three-dimensional effect.

Diag. 24 *Briar roses in bobbin lace*

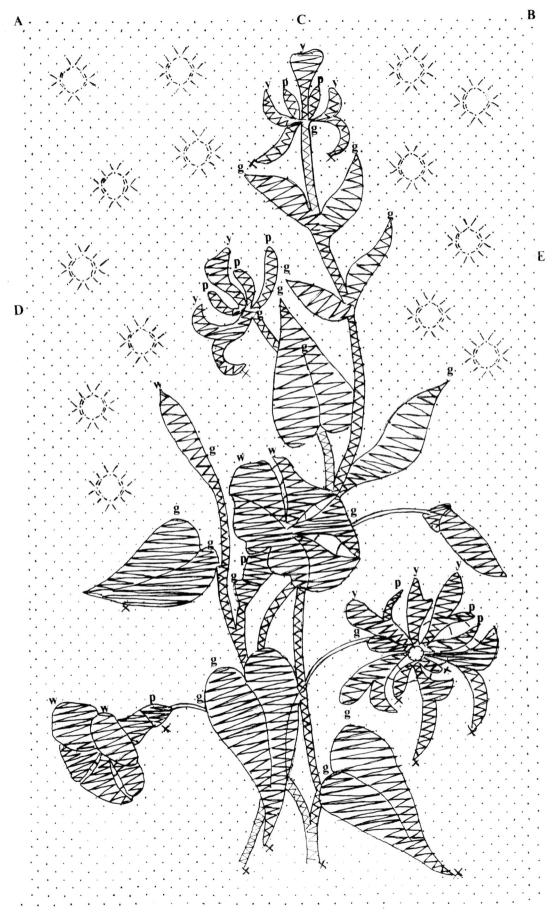

Diag. 25
*Honeysuckle
and bindweed
in bobbin lace*

Honeysuckle and bindweed

Materials required
64 prs white (w), 8 prs yellow (y), 10 prs pink (p), 17 prs green (g).

Method
Start in the same way as for the roses, hanging two pairs on each pinhole through two pairs of

passives from **A** to **B**. Establish the Torchon ground with holes from **C** to **D** and **C** to **E**.

Beginning with the honeysuckle, use pink for the closed buds and yellow for the open flowers as indicated; carry the pink pair into the stalk, weave with green for 1cm ($\frac{3}{8}$in) then remove it.

Work the honeysuckle leaves, taking the extra green pairs into the stalk. Work the second honeysuckle flower in pink and yellow as indicated; bring these into the last open petal to give a mingling of colours. At this stage continue the honeysuckle stalk and begin the first convolvulus leaf. Divide after 2cm ($\frac{13}{16}$in), add another green pair and finish the leaf in two parts, meeting the green weavers.

Work the last honeysuckle leaf and the convolvulus bud.

Add extra white pairs as indicated and work the convolvulus flower, leaving pairs out to make small plaits to join the petals.

Add two green pairs and use like a gimp to make the curved stalk for the second bud.

Work the second convolvulus leaf in two parts; make the top half and leave pairs out for the lower half.

Work the last honeysuckle flower leaving a small hole in the centre and add two green pairs for the curved stalk.

Make the third convolvulus leaf in two parts as in the first leaf, and make the last convolvulus leaf like the second. Add two green pairs for the second convolvulus's curved stalk and make the flower. Continue to the base and gradually take threads into the lower edge.

Carrickmacross
Trace off the design without the net dots and work as in chapter 2.

Needlelace
The design cannot be worked in needlelace without a great deal of adaptation.

Fig. 17 Honeysuckle and bindweed representing August

Daffodils and snowdrops

Materials required
62 prs white (w), 14 prs green (g), 10 prs yellow (y)
(random thread dyed yellow is suitable).

Add coloured pairs at the letters indicated and
remove them at **X**.

Method
Start at **A** and make a braid with five pairs to **B**,
hanging two pairs at each pinhole on the inside
of the braid. Start another braid at **A** with five
pairs for the left-hand side; this braid is worked
in conjunction with the ground. Establish the
ground **C** to **D** and **C** to **E**. Work the top leaf and
save the green pair to take over the flower for
the stalk.

Make the top petal of the daffodil with a twist to
the centre for veining; start the second leaf and
work it in conjuction with the second petal. On
the left, work the third petal edge simultaneously with its turn-back edge and the calyx
with its small pointed leaf.

Use a yellow pair from the upper petals to work
the trumpet and use a new green pair as a gimp
to divide the inner and outer surfaces. Bring the
other yellow pairs through to make the lower
petals. Work each of the three centre stalks
independently, joining their weavers at intervals to hold them together.

Start each snowdrop leaf with green and carry
the threads into the other leaves. Cut off the
snowdrop calyx green pair before starting the
petals. Where there is a curved stalk, use a
green pair as a gimp and take it through the
ground to use in working the calyx.

Make the other daffodil as the first. Start this
daffodil's lower leaf with two green pairs so that
the turn back can be achieved.

Gradually take out the green pairs that
accumulate, finish the ground threads into the
bottom braid and join and tie off at **F**.

Carrickmacross
Trace the outline of the design and work as in
chapter 2. Darn the reverse side in two shades

Fig. 18 *Daffodils and snowdrops
representing March*

of green and three shades of yellow. Leave the
snowdrops white.

Needlelace
Trace the outline of the design and work as in
chapter 2. Use open stitches – pea stitch, single
or double Brussels – for the daffodil petals. Work
the trumpet solid in corded Brussels stitch.

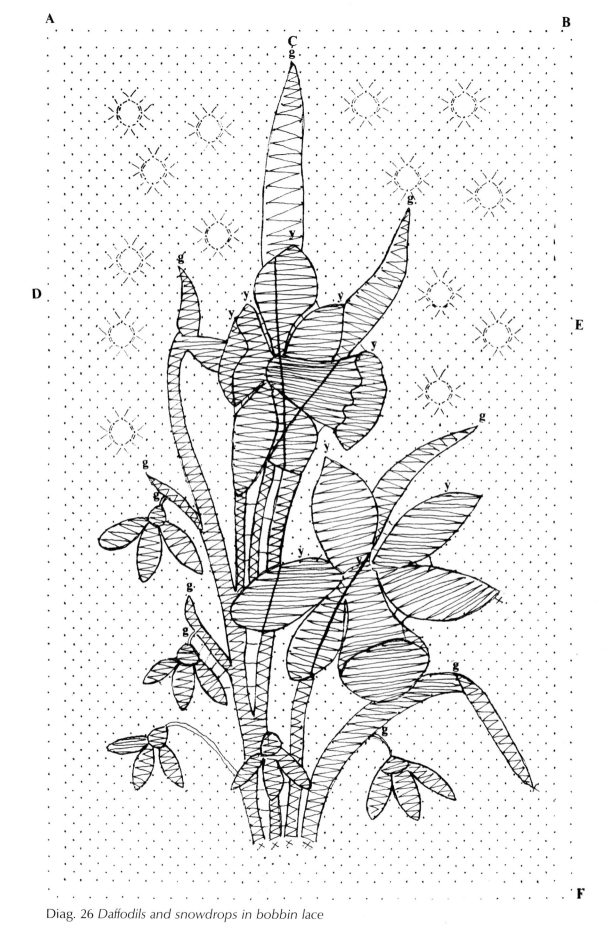

Diag. 26 *Daffodils and snowdrops in bobbin lace*

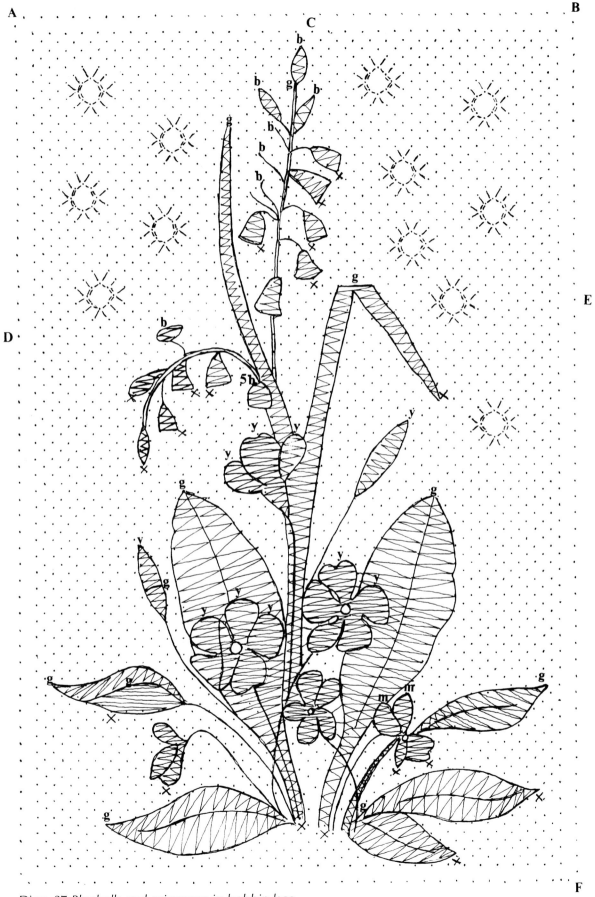

Diag. 27 *Bluebells and primroses in bobbin lace*

Fig. 19 *Bluebells, primroses and violets representing April*

Bluebell, primroses and violets

Materials required
64 prs white (w), 10 prs blue (b), 3 shades of green (5, 8, and 6 prs) (g), 10 prs yellow (y), 6 prs mauve (m).

Add coloured pairs at the letters indicated and remove them at **X**. This uses more colours and the large number of blue pairs needs only small amounts of thread.

Method
Begin as for the daffodils with a braid, and establish the ground from **C** to **D** and **C** to **E**, working the braid down either side.

Work the top bell and use the blue pair and a green pair as a gimp stalk. As more pairs of blue are introduced, carry them along in this stalk until they are needed to work the other bells.

Work the bluebell leaf, and then the second spray, which has 1 pr green and 5 prs blue taken through as a gimp from the leaf side. Use 2 prs green for the folded-over leaf, light for the main part and darker for the turn back.

Make the three primrose petals and carry the pairs through the calyx; keep them together when weaving the stalk so that they appear to belong to the primrose.

Work the primrose leaves in two halves, with the weavers meeting each time at the centre. In conjunction with the leaves, work the petals of the other primroses.

Sew in a bead for the flowers' centres.

Work each lower leaf in two parts. For the violet stalks, bunch the mauve and green threads together and treat as a gimp. Finish the threads into the bottom braid, join and cut off at **F**.

Carrickmacross
Trace the outline of the design and work as in chapter 2. Darn in the appropriate colours.

Needlelace
This needs some adaptation; enlarge the bluebells to make them workable. The primrose leaves can be worked complete and the flowers worked separately and superimposed to give dimension.

Fig. 20 *Butterfly in Bedfordshire techniques*

Diag. 28 *Butterfly in bobbin lace*

BUTTERFLY
(using Bedfordshire techniques)
The use of Bedfordshire leaves and plaits make it possible to use different colours. This one has been worked in ten shades of one colour plus gold. Gold seems to look better with dark, hot colours and silver with the pale, cool colours.

The body
Start at the antennae, each with 4 prs and work a small braid of Honiton rib to the head. Work the 8 prs in cloth stitch for the head, change to half-stitch for the thorax and then go back to cloth stitch for the lower body. At the tip work down to the head again so that a double body is formed. Tie off.

The wings

Sew in 2 prs gold and a thick gold thread and work from **A** to **B** adding 2 prs as indicated for plaits and petals. Add 2 prs of the coloured threads at **B** to widen the outer edge. Incoming leaves will increase this as the work proceeds. Follow the arrows on the wing diagram, making windmill crossings.

Work the flower centres in half stitch and sew the plaits into the body where necessary.

At the lower wing **C**, use 2 prs gold to work the plait backwards and forwards to either side of the wing, sewing into the body. The coloured threads end in the band of cloth stitch down to **D**, resulting in an interesting blend of colours. Take out pairs from this edge as they accumulate, to leave 4 prs at the tip, tie off and darn them back. Work the other wing in the same way.

While still on the pillow, take the lower body over the top of the other one, tuck in the threads and sew together. A thick gold thread may be sewn to the edge for emphasis.

This can be applied to a garment, framed as a picture or, with wire added to the outer edge, can be made free standing.

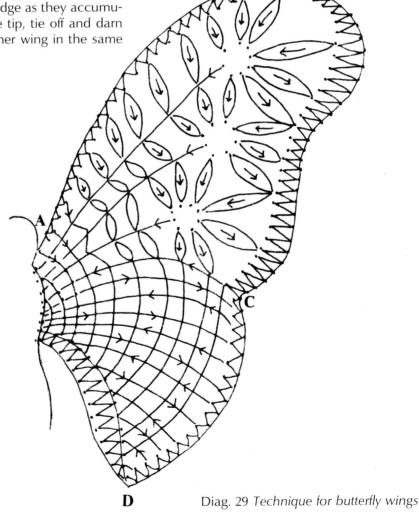

Diag. 29 *Technique for butterfly wings*

Fig. 21 *Rabbits in a pine wood, using Torchon and Bedfordshire techniques*

RABBITS IN BOBBIN LACE

Materials required
50 sylko, Spécial Dentelles, DMC Broder Machine 30 are all suitable. 10 prs blue, 31 prs white, 6 prs bright green for the ground and 8 prs dark green, 4 prs brown for the coloured weavers.

This design is worked in shades of green, blue, and dark brown. The overall ground is white, but if the ground stitch used is whole-stitch Torchon the background colours will stay in place as stripes. The brown thread used for the tree trunks is carried through the trees out into the ground as a fence, and is then used for the rabbits.

The design can be used as a repeat pattern – on a lamp base or shade, an inset on a cloth, table mat, cushion or cot cover.

Method
On each pinhole, set up 2 prs blue from **A** to **B** (10 prs), 2 prs white from **B** to **C** (28 prs), 2 prs bright green from **C** to **D** (6 prs) and 3 prs white on **D**.

Add coloured weavers at **0** as indicated and remove them at **X**. Weave the dark-green pairs through white pairs on each tree branch meeting the weavers from the lower branches and the brown pair from the trunk. Drop out pairs for each consecutive branch as indicated. Work the smaller trees in the same way. Introduce new green weavers for each tree branch and cut them off at the branch ends.

Work daisies in the form of Maltese leaves below the trees, as indicated.

Carry the threads from the tree trunk along the lower branches into the ground; use them to work the rabbits.

The rabbits
Start the body and head of the first rabbit with the brown pairs and meet the weavers where the body joins the head.

Work Maltese leaves for the ears, using one brown pair and one ground pair, taking them into the head and out again into the ground.

Carry the brown pair along to work the second rabbit's head.

Carry any white threads which appear surplus over the back of the ears to continue in the ground.

The tails
Work these in the Bedfordshire technique.

Take two pairs of white passives from the base of the rabbit and make a square tally (weave 6 or 8 times).

Bring the pairs back in to the rabbit body and carry on weaving with the brown. Pull the tallies through to the other side when the panel is complete.

If joining into a circle for a lamp, begin as indicated on the centre line of a tree. If using for a cushion or flat inset, begin at the tips of the large tree branches.

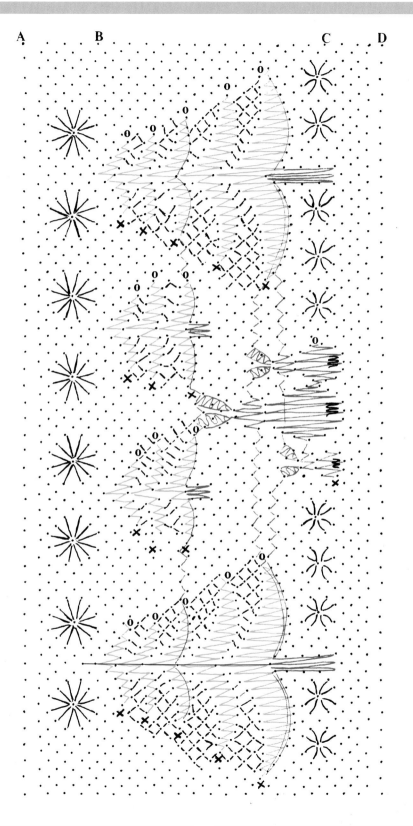

A   B   C   D

Diag. 30
*Rabbits in
bobbin lace*

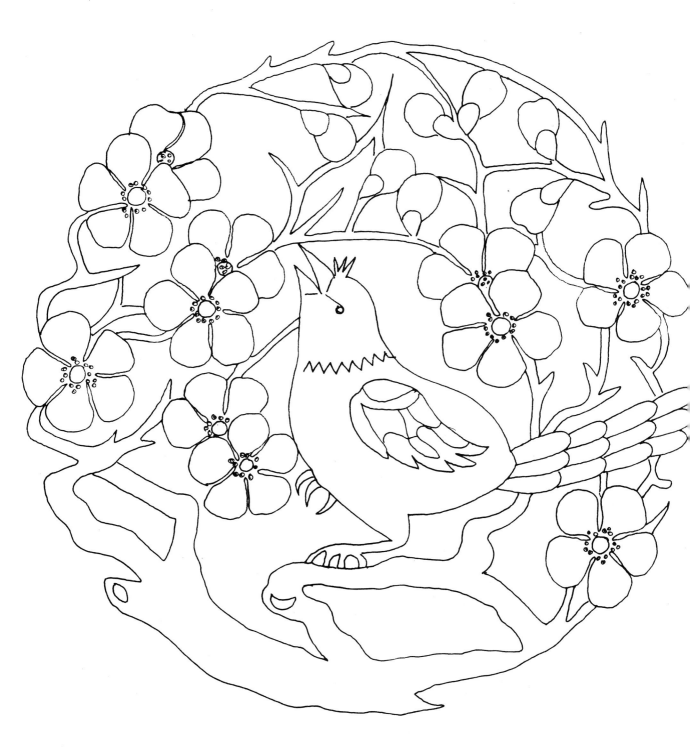

Diag. 31 *Carrickmacross cushion or panel*

Diag. 32 Carrickmacross cushion or panel

Fig. 22 *Carrickmacross cushion*

CARRICKMACROSS CUSHION

The two bird designs are taken from Chinese paper cuts – this source is very useful for Carrickmacross as many of the designs need little or no alteration except perhaps to enlarge them.

Materials required for each cushion
A circle of net 36cm (14in) in diameter, a circle of organdie 20cm (8in) in diameter, stranded cotton in 3 shades of pink, 3 shades of blue/green, yellow and brown, 0.5m (19½in) each of pink cotton material and grey cotton material.

Method

Bird 1
Trace the design, and place it in the centre of the net circle. Work the Carrickmacross as in chapter 2, and on completion cut away the organdie from the inner design and at the outer edge.

Darn the flowers in pink, varying the shades – darker for those in the background. Darn the bird's body in brown and the wings and tail in blue/green.

Work the surface stitchery on the bird, and French knots in the centres of the flowers. Make a few stitches in yellow for the beak.

Bird 2
Work the Carrickmacross as before, cut away the organdie within the design and the outer edge, and also the inner veins on the leaves.

Darn the flowers in pink with the darker shade at the top of the bell. Darn the leaves in blue/green and the bird in brown with surface fly stitch. Work stem stitch on the flowers.

To make the cushion
Cut out a 36cm (14in) circle in grey and another in pink. Cut crossway strips 6cm (2½in) wide from the pink cotton, join them to make a 2m (6ft 7in) length and form into a circle. Fold over to make a 3cm (1⅜in) double frill and gather to fit the circle.

Tack the net to the grey circle and the folded frill round the edge; folded edge to the centre.

Place the pink circle on top and machine through all the layers leaving a small gap for the stuffing. Turn through to the right side and stuff.

Cushions in Carrickmacross are decorative and suitable for bedrooms, alternatively, this design looks attractive as a picture, or under a glass tray.

Needlelace
The design can be worked in needlelace following the instructions in chapter 2.

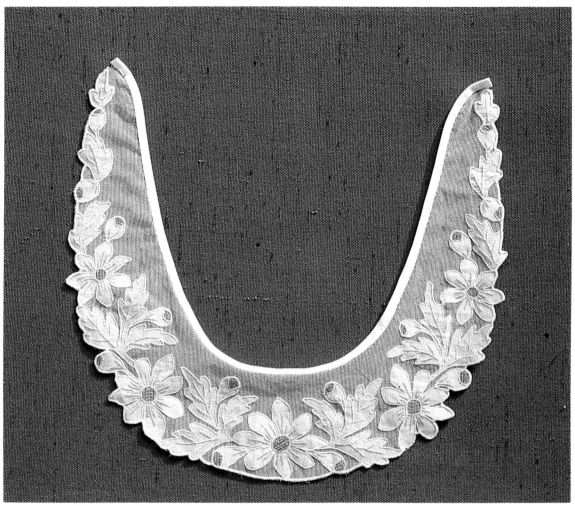

Fig. 23 *Carrickmacross daisy collar darned in shades of orange and green*

DAISY COLLAR IN CARRICKMACROSS

Trace the pattern to make a whole collar, **C/D** is the centre back, join **A/B** to **A/B**. Trace the dotted-line neck edge.

Work the Carrickmacross as described in chapter 2 and work close loop stitch round the outer edge to make it firm. Trim the organdie back to this edge.

Make a tack line to indicate the neck edge and trim away the organdie from the inner design.

Darn the flower petals; these may be shaded by working the darning in two or three colours.

Work fillings in the buds and the centres of the flowers following *Diag. 21*. Use stem stitch for the veining on leaves and petals.

Attach bias binding to the neck edge.

Needlelace
Trace the design and prepare as described in chapter 2. Work the flowers and leaves as for the clematis and, to hold the lace together, work bars as in *Diag. 35*; alternatively apply it to machine net. If applied to a dress neckline no background is needed.

Diags 33a & b *Daisy collar in Carrickmacross or needlelace (enlarge by 10%)*

Diag. 34 *Poppy inset in needlelace
(enlarge by 10%)*

DRESS INSET IN NEEDLELACE

This poppy design was inspired by a cornfield in summer, with daisies, poppies and cornflowers. One design was made into a fan and the other into an inset for an evening dress, the leaves hang free over the edge of the U-shaped neckline.

The working chart for needlelace stitches

Heavy outlines indicate top stitching, light lines indicate the outlining and dotted lines indicate the direction of the stitches.

a is corded Brussels stitch p. 13
b is pea stitch p. 14
c is double Brussels stitch p. 88
d is Brussels stitch p. 13
e is corded Brussels stitch with holes p. 13
f is beading p. 88
g is Point de Venise p. 89
h is pyramid stitch p. 88
j is Point de Gaze p. 89
k is Alençon p. 89

This chart should be referred to for all needle-lace patterns in this book.

Fig. 24 *Needlelace dress inset*

Method

Trace the design and reverse it to make the complete oval.

Couch red threads for the poppies, green for the leaves and white for the daisies, making sure that all these threads are attached to one another.

Work in rotation: start with the poppies, next loop the green threads for the leaves and then the white for the daisy. Use the ends of these couched threads to start the fillings.

Work the leaves in corded Brussels stitch as for the clematis leaves (*p. 11*) with top-stitched veins, some in light green and some in mid-green. Work some of the poppy petals in corded Brussels stitch and some in pea stitch as indicated in *Diag. 34*. Use bars and spider wheels to fill spaces (*Diags 35 & 36*).

Work green couronnes in the centres of the poppies with bullion knots in black for the stamens.

Work the daisies with a centre vein of corded Brussels stitch with holes.

Do not work the top stitching till the centre net is applied.

The centre net

Tack a piece of net (navy blue or black) over the centre oval on the right side and work the top stitching through this and the design.

Finally, trim away the excess net from the flowers and leaves, close to the stitching. The net is held much more firmly than if the design had been applied.

Fig. 25 *Fan made representing Summer*

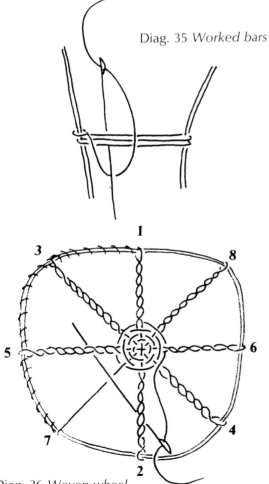

Diag. 35 *Worked bars*

Diag. 36 *Woven wheel*

Worked bars

Take the thread across the space three times and buttonhole stitch over it.

Spider or woven wheels

These are useful for filling in a circular or oval space.

Take the thread across the space from **1** to **2**, whip back over the thread to **1**.

Whip along the outline to the next strut at **3**, cross to **4** and back, whip along from **3** to **5**, **5** to **6** and back, **5** to **7** and **7** to **8**.
Whip back as far as the centre and complete the wheel by darning in and out of the struts. Since there is an even number of struts, it is necessary to work over two and under one periodically. Do not work this in the same place each time. Finally whip back to **7**.

If you cannot draw from life, take flower shapes from books, seed catalogues or any other flower pictures. It is the composition of the design which needs particular care. Arrange the flowers in a pleasing shape and then decide on the colour. 'Paint up' the design so that the balance of colour and shape can be appreciated and, if necessary, adjusted. Try to match the colours as closely as possible to the threads that you propose to use. This balance is very important in all-over design such as the fan.

BUTTERFLIES IN NEEDLELACE

Materials required
Stranded cotton, silk 100/3, 50 sylko, DMC Spécial Dentelles.

Butterflies are a favourite with lace-makers and have been portrayed in lace for centuries. They can be used on dresses, in flower pictures, on evening bags, as brooches or hair decorations, etc.

It is possible to take a butterfly shape and then design fillings to fit, but it is more interesting to make butterflies in needlelace exactly as they appear in nature. The following eight patterns are British butterflies and the shape, colour and markings are copied from life. The techniques are adapted to make them look realistic.

All the butterflies have a mid-grey outline; this accommodates the colour changes and shows through the other stitchery as a guide to top stitching, they can also act as faint vein lines.

Couch the outlining thread on every line as continuously as possible, starting at the antennae. For a free-standing butterfly, add fine fuse wire with the final top stitching on the outer edge only. Overcast the wire to the outside edge, add two more threads and top stitch as before. Check the colours from a butterfly illustration when selecting threads and use the *Working chart for needlelace stitches (p. 53)*.

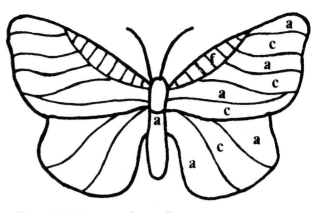

Diag. 38 *Brimstone butterfly*

The Orange Tip

The stitches used are indicated in *Diag. 37*. Outline the body and wing edges in grey and the inner wing lines in white.

Work the body in mid-grey and the wings in white with orange tips.

Top stitch the edges – mid-grey for the white parts and dark grey for the orange.

The Brimstone

Follow *Diag. 38* for the stitches. Outline the body and wing edges in mid-grey and the inner wing lines in yellow.

Work the wings in random-dyed yellow thread, making sure that both sides match.

Top stitch the body and wing edges in mid-grey.

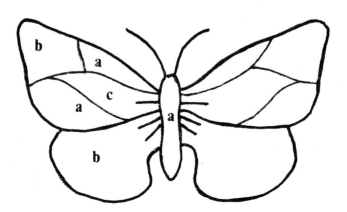

Diag. 37 *Orange Tip butterfly*

Diag. 39 *Swallowtail butterfly*

The Swallowtail

In dark grey, outline all the design lines and fill the corded Brussels stitch areas of the top wing.

Work the lower wings with bands of turquoise and yellow at the edges and mid-grey near the body.

Fill the body with dark grey and the other areas with yellow. Fill the red spots on the lower wings.

Top stitch the 'figure of eight' at the top outer edge of the wings in yellow, by laying four threads and whipping them into place; buttonhole stitch each ring individually.

Top stitch all vein lines and outer edges in dark grey.

The Purple Emperor

Outline in mid-grey and work the blue over these lines so that they show through for the final top stitching.

Work mid-grey for the outer edges of the wings and the body.

Top stitch all the lines as indicated in the diagram and make white couronnes for the spots.

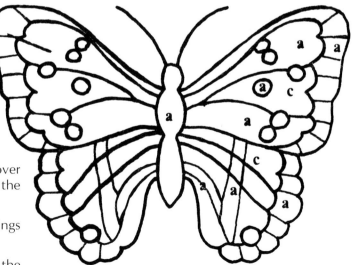

Diag. 40 *Purple Emperor butterfly*

Fig. 26 *Unfinished needlace with Peacock and Purple Emperor butterflies. Architect's linen, outlining thread and partly worked fillings can be seen*

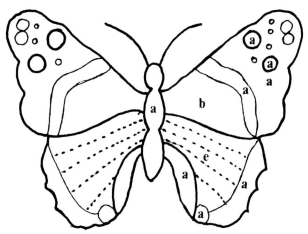

Diag. 41 *Red Admiral butterfly (enlarge by 10%)*

The Red Admiral

Outline and work the top wing tip in dark grey with some spots in white. Use orange/red for the inner bands and light grey on the lower wing with a blue spot.

Work the other areas in black following the dotted guide lines.

Work the corded Brussels stitch with holes and two rows of corded Brussels stitch in between.

Top stitch the body, the wings and some of the white spots in black, and add white couronnes and blue French knots for the other spots.

The Peacock

The internal colours are not top stitched and the veining is only faintly apparent through the outlining.

Outline in mid-grey and top stitch in dark grey. Work the top wing in orange/red with some blocks of grey; work the 'eyes' in yellow with red and grey centres.

Work the lower wing in mid-grey and brown, with the 'eyes' in light blue and pale yellow.

Fig. 27 Orange Tip butterfly lightly attached to the panel in Fig. 7

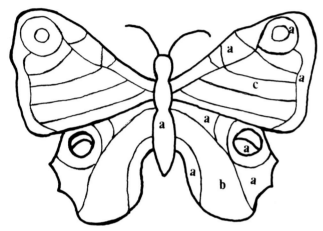

Diag. 42 Peacock butterfly (enlarge by 10%)

Fig. 28 The Tortoiseshell, Milkweed, Brimstone, Red Admiral and Swallowtail butterflies

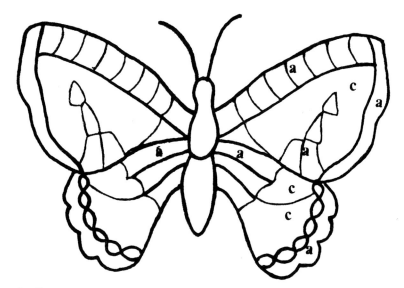

The Tortoiseshell

Outline in mid-grey and work the blocks of corded Brussels stitch on the upper wings in stripes of yellow, red and dark grey.

Work the outer edge and the areas close to the body in mid-grey and make the 'figure of eight' on the lower wing in blue, top stitched in dark grey.

Top stitch the heavy lined areas in dark grey.

Diag. 43 *Tortoiseshell butterfly*

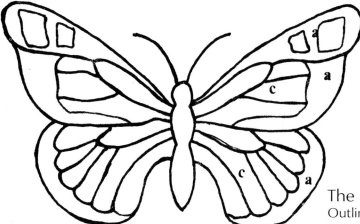

Diag. 44 *Milkweed butterfly*

The Milkweed

Outline in dark grey and work the corded Brussels stitch on the upper wings in dark grey with orange patches.

Work the double Brussels stitch over the outlines to fill the wings, and top stitch the veins and edges in dark grey.

Diag. 45 *Briar-rose spray for Carrickmacross or needlelace*

Fig. 29 *Needlelace rose spray*

NEEDLELACE ROSES

Materials required
As for butterflies (p. 56).
Follow the *Working chart for needlelace stitches*
(*p. 53*).

This small spray is wired on the outside edge
and has an extra flower worked and applied at **X**
afterwards.

Work the flowers in white then top stitch in pink.

Work the corded Brussels stitch in the petals in
rows to the centre as shown by the dotted lines,
but work some rows only halfway, taking the
laid thread through one of the previous loops
instead of the outer edge as is usual. This forms
triangular wedges and is an easy way of filling up
this unusual petal shape. The technique works
bests in corded Brussels stitch but it can be used
in other, more open stitches.

The spray makes a decorative corsage; it can be
applied to a prayer book or on a bride's shoes,
worn as a hair decoration or mounted on the
edge of a photograph frame.

CONVOLVULUS FAN IN NEEDLELACE

Materials required
Use 50 sylko or cotton, silk 100/3.

This pattern can be made into a fan or yoke, or
applied to a neck edge. It can be mounted on
net or, for bobbin lace makers, can have a
bobbin net background.
  The upper part is held together with bars and
needs no net. Some of the flowers have extra
petals and these should be completed first.

Method
Follow the *Working chart for needlelace stitches*
(*p. 53*).

Match the two pattern parts **A/B** to **A/B**; trace
and outline in the usual way.

Use the triangular wedge method (*p. 62*) for the
flowers and maintain the rows as indicated by
the dotted lines.

The central circles are either pink couronnes or
a pink 'figure of eight'. These flowers may, if

required, be shaded using a white-threaded needle and a pink-threaded needle simultaneously, sometimes working half-way across the flower in pink and then completely across in white. This can be done entirely at random, shading as you work.

Radiate the pink rows from the centre as shown. The leaves are in a pale green and a random dyed green thread works well.

Work all the bars and couronnes before top stitching; add the extra petals and top stitch them to the relevant flower so that they appear continuous.

The finished spray can be applied to net or the net can be applied with the top stitching as in the poppy inset (p. 54).

For bobbin lace makers

Work a net ground on to the completed needlelace sprays using the following method.

Make another pattern in reverse with the needle parts in outline and the dots for the ground. Place this on the pillow, with card under if it is on tracing paper, and pin the needlelace in the correct position, upside-down with the wrong side facing.

Sew (as in Honiton sewings) pairs into the needlelace — this can be done with a fine crochet hook working into, or just inside the top stitching.

Add pairs as you need them, take them out into the needlelace and tie them off when they are no longer needed. Sometimes it is possible to carry them across the work to use again and this works very well as the needlelace is solid enough not to show the threads.

The dotted ground is for Torchon but any fancy stitch can be used and the dots marked in at the angle shown.

Fig. 30 *Convolvulus fan in needlelace with a bobbin lace background*

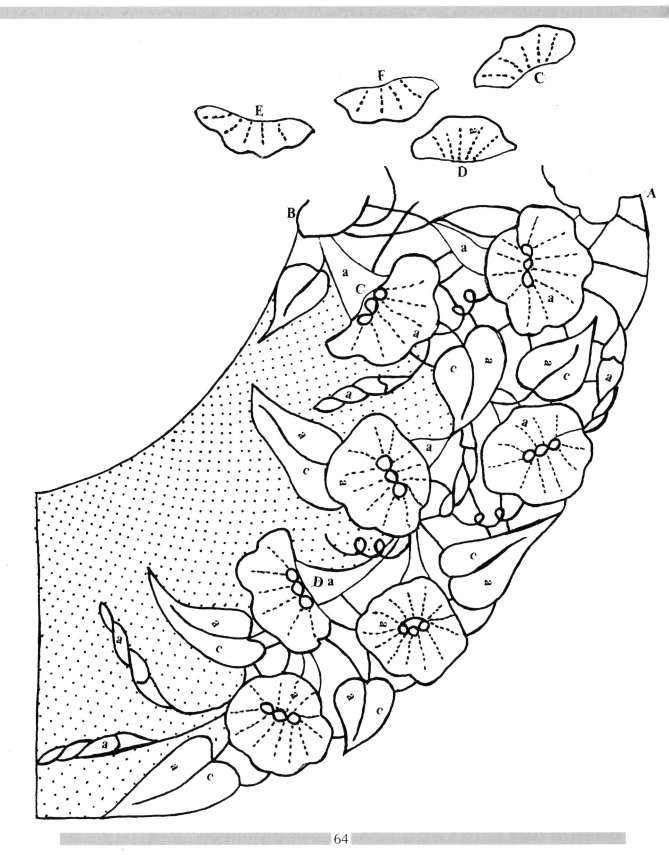

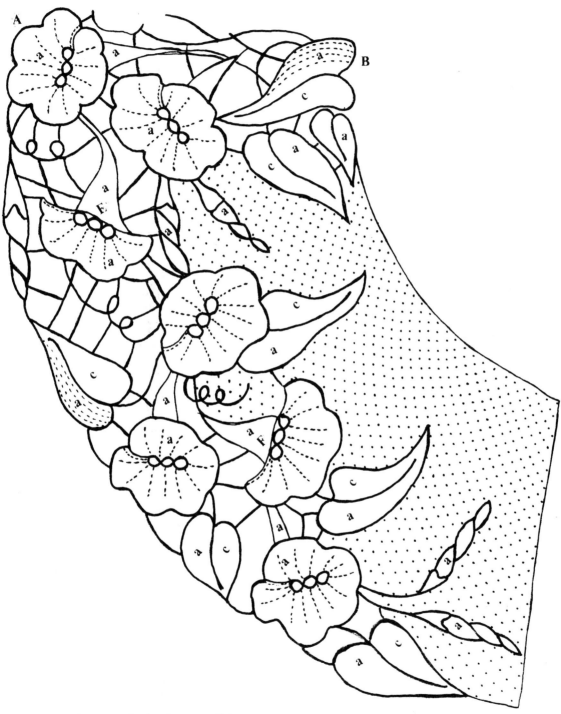

Diags 46a & b *Convolvulus fan, needlelace or Carrickmacross (enlarge by 10%)*

Fig. 31 *Carrickmacross fan from* Diag. 47

CARRICKMACROSS FAN

Trace off the pattern from *Diag. 47* and reverse it to form a half circle, or a whole circle if you want to make a collar or mat.

Work as for Carrickmacross in chapter 2 but make a picot edge as in *Diag. 20* and trim the organdie to this edge.

Darn the leaves and flowers in bright colours and work stem stitch for the veining and French knots at the flower centres.

Needlelace

This design can be made in needlelace but the working thread must be very fine to show the detail. It is therefore advisable to enlarge it and use thicker threads.

The completed design can be worked with buttonholed bars to hold the parts together or it can be mounted on net.

To mount the lace on fan sticks
Spread the sticks to fit the lace and paint them with a resin glue.

Allow to dry and then iron the lace on to the sticks through a clean dry cloth.

Fig. 32 *Brooch and earrings*

NEEDLELACE JEWELLERY

Needlelace makes a solid construction, especially when a metallic thread is used. It needs to be top stitched with a silver wire incorporated. The patterns given here also have added gem stones.

The working method is as for all needlelace but when the wire is added to the top stitching it is advisable to whip the wire to the outlining first, and then top stitch over it and a further four threads.

Follow the *Working chart for needlelace stitches* (p. 53) and use materials as for Butterflies (p. 56) with the addition of DMC Spécial Dentelles gold or Madeira gold.

Fig. 33 *The bees made as a necklace*

Diag. 47 *Fan in Carrickmacross*
(enlarge by 10%)

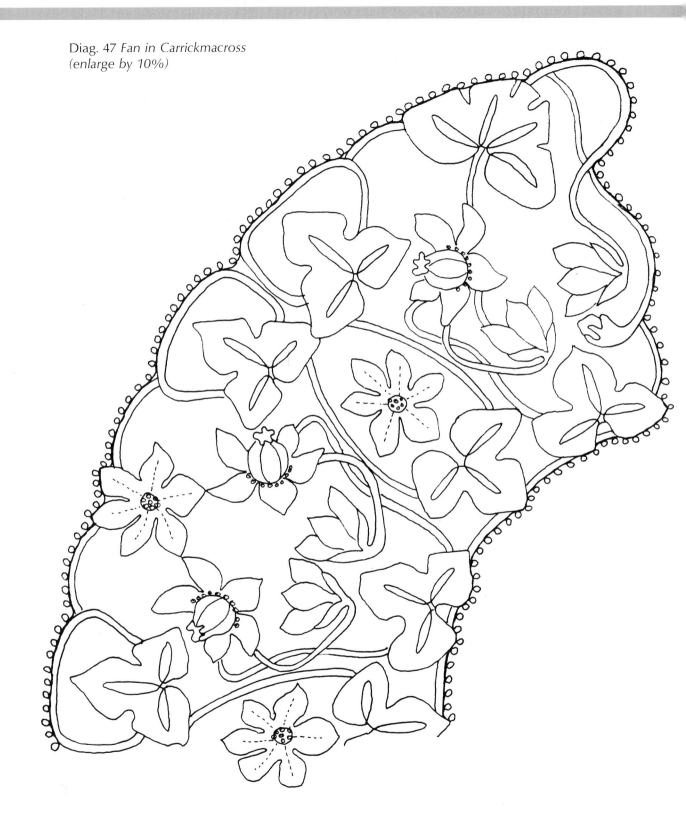

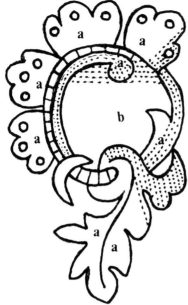

Diag. 48 *Brooch and earrings in needlelace (enlarge by 10%)*

Brooch and earrings

The design was taken from an antique piece of Venetian needlelace.

Method

Outline in a dark-yellow thread round the entire design and work as indicated in *Diag. 48*. Most of the areas are worked in gold but the coloured area can be made to match particular items of clothing.

Top stitch as indicated using wire at the outer edge only.

Make 13 couronnes in a coloured thread and attach them to the leaf. These form 'nests' in which to glue the gem stones.

Make three small flowers without a wire surround, attach couronnes to the centres and use one on the brooch and the other two for earrings.

Glue them to studs and add the gem stones. Sew a pin to the reverse side of the brooch.

The bees

Materials required

DMC Spécial Dentelles Gold or Madeira Gold and as for butterflies.

This motif can be made into a brooch or necklace; the idea was taken from a piece of Egyptian tomb jewellery.

Method

Outline as before in dark yellow and work in gold with brown silk for the body stripes. Top stitch with gold thread and heavy wire as described for the previous brooch.

The pollen ball is made of five couronnes attached to the round centre which is worked as a woven wheel and filled with amber gem stones. The eyes are red couronnes with diamond gems.

If a necklace is required, allow the wire to form loops at the top to accommodate a neck chain.

Diag. 49 *Bees in needlelace (enlarge by 10%)*

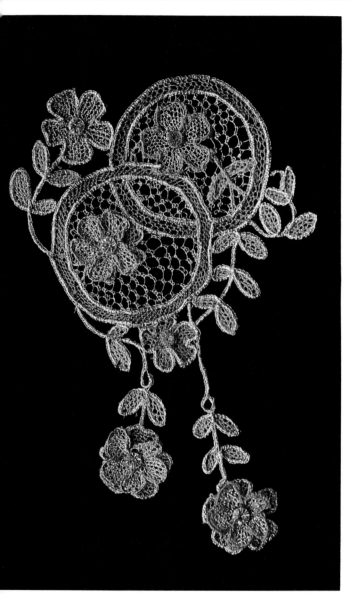

Fig. 34 *Rings and flowers necklace*

The ring and flower necklace
This was inspired by a piece of antique jewellery and is worked in silver, turquoise and green.

Method

Follow the diagram for the stitches and attach a heavy wire round the outer edge, including all the drop leaf sprays.

Make five flowers as in *Diag. 48*, add three more to give dimension to the brooch and a further two for matching earrings.

Make couronnes for all the flower centres and add diamond gems to them.

A silver chain may be attached through the wire edge.

Diag. 50 *Necklace in needlelace*

4. Themes in lace

Constructing a piece of lace is sometimes prompted or inspired by an evocative theme – a poem, a book, a particular time of the year, a holiday, an event, etc. Themes are sometimes set for examination design questions or assessments and also for competitions. The use of colour in such pieces has to be carefully planned to make an overall balanced piece of work. Sometimes the colours are mentioned in the book or poem but often they are not.

The Harvest scene in *Fig. 1* uses autumn colours, and it entailed constructing a design of fruits and vegetables that appear at harvest time for both people and animals. A fan needs a firm outside edge which has to be incorporated into the design, and it was decided that a grapevine on one side could be balanced by

Fig. 35 *Mediaeval Panel:*
  'One I love, two I love, three I love I say,
  Four I love with all my heart, five I cast away'

runner beans on the other. Similarly, the yellow apples and pears are balanced by marrows and their yellow flowers, for the balance has to be in both the shapes and the colours. The wild rose rambles along the base, interspersed with blackberries and hazelnuts, the red rosehips adding a splash of colour. The whole, though balanced, is not symmetrical. The grey church in bobbin lace is intended as a misty scene in the distance.

Bright, warm colours are used for the Poppy fan in *Fig. 25* to create the impression of a hot summer day.

Awareness is required, not only of colour harmony as discussed in chapter 1, but also of the design principles listed in chapter 3. Together, these will show the way to approach a complicated piece of work, and the eye will help discern what 'looks right'. The end purpose of the lace will dictate the design and the colours should be 'painted up' to make quite sure that the balance is correct.

Diags 51a, b & c
*Mediaeval figures
in needlelace*

Fig. 36 *Close up of the mediaeval panel*

MEDIAEVAL FIGURES IN NEEDLELACE

The idea came from a skipping rhyme illustrated on a tea towel.

A varied colour scheme was chosen, with dresses to match hair colours and to harmonize with the adjacent figures. First of all, the colours for one of the characters must be chosen. The 'Gay Gallant', the central figure, is in mauve and yellow, with white shirt and brown hair. One adjacent lady is in green, with red hair, and a blonde on the opposite side is in turquoise and dark red. The black-haired lady in browns and yellows is next to the one in green, and the dark-haired lady in pink and white is next to the one in turquoise. The dogs – greyhounds – are in their natural colours. The 'cast-off' lady is in blue and red, with brown hair, the colours emphasizing that she is separate from the rest.

Fig. 37 *Close up of the mediaeval panel*

The wimples have no top stitching and are worked in a finer thread to impart a soft appearance. There are no features on the faces; this is optional, but embroidery sometimes makes them look unrealistic.

The rose tree is in natural colours with heavy, brown threads for the trunk and branches, random-dyed green thread for the leaves and random-dyed pink for the flowers. Shading is achieved by using these random-dyed threads. Fuse wire is added to the final top stitching of these so that they can be moulded to give dimension. The ground is strewn with butter-cups and daisies.

The threads are mainly silk 100/3 but there is some sylko 50 and Fil à Dentelle.

The *Working chart for needlelace stitches* (p. 53) should be followed.

Diag. 52 *Alice*

Fig. 38 *Alice's Adventures in Wonderland*

ALICE IN WONDERLAND

This is made into a fan and therefore requires firm outer and lower edges in the design. (For the purposes of this book, the fan has been broken down into its various individual scenes.) To achieve this, the scene is portrayed in a wood, the intertwined branches forming the top edge, with leaves at intervals to fill the spaces, and the lower edge consisting of 'painted roses'. Spaces are created between the trees to accommodate the characters from the story.

The colours

The threads used are silks 100/3, sylko 50 and Fil à Dentelle.

The muted colours of the natural woodland enable the figures to be worked in the strong, primary colours found in playing-cards. The design of the figures and the patterning on their clothing has also been taken from playing cards.

Balancing the colours was interesting: the toadstool had to be red to balance the red roses on the opposite side; all the characters are in red, yellow, blue and black, except for Alice who needs to be different.

The whole is mounted on black net so that the figures stand out.

The following diagrams illustrate the characters to be made into small pictures. Alice and the King and Queen fit together to make a larger picture, or they can be worked separately.

The *Working chart for needlelace stitches* (*p. 53*) should be used for working the pieces.

Alice

Dress – mid-blue with a white apron.
Hair – shiny yellow.
Shoes – black.
Stockings – white.
The flamingo – salmon pink, top stitched in pink and black.
The hedgehog – dark grey with mid-grey spikes in top stitching.

'A Cat may look at a King'

The Cat

Random-dyed yellow/orange thread, solid face and paws and open stitches for the body.
Eyes – green with black centres, no top stitching.

The King

Dress – random-dyed blue with plain white border, top stitched in yellow, and hearts worked by one fly stitch on top of the other (embroidered afterwards).
Collar – white with blue 'lazy daisies' embroidered afterwards.
Belt – white with black herringbone.
Shoes – red with white couronnes for pompons.
Hair – grey, top stitched in black.

Fig. 39 *'Just as she had the flamingo's neck nicely straightened out, it would twist itself round and look into her face'*

'A cat may look at a King', said Alice

Diag. 53 *'A cat may look at a King'*

Diag. 54 *The Queen and Knave of Hearts*

The Queen of Hearts

Skirt – random-dyed blue with white bands top stitched in yellow with red fly stitch for the hearts. Yellow top stitching and 'lazy daisies' form the centre border.

Sleeves – blue with white borders and red fly stitch hearts.

Bodice – red with a yellow inset and white collar top stitched in black.

The Knave

Dress – random-dyed blue with a border of fly stitch hearts on white and black herringbone on yellow.

Tarts – red, top stitched in pale yellow.

Fig. 40 *'The Queen of Hearts, she made some tarts,*
All on a summer's day,
The Knave of Hearts, he stole the tarts,
and took them quite away'

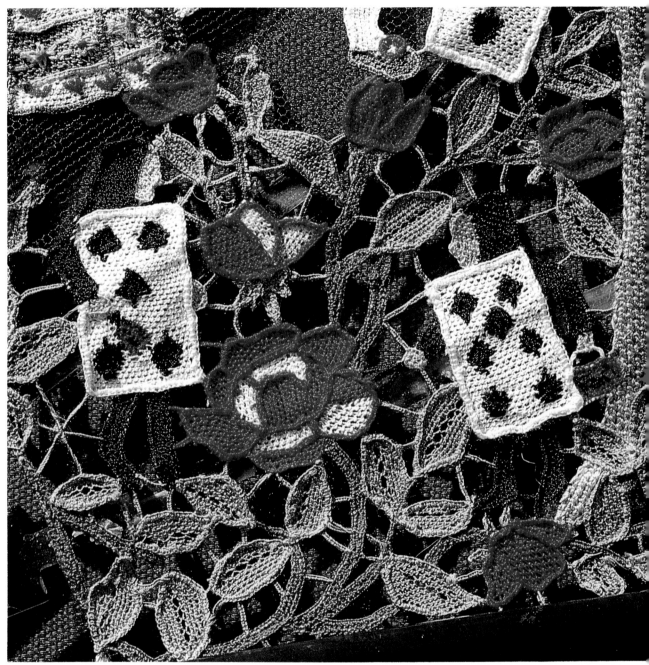

Fig. 41 *'Would you tell me please', said Alice, 'Why you are painting those roses'*

The playing cards

The hearts, diamonds and spades are out-lined, filled in corded Brussels stitch, but not top stitched. The small areas are joined to one another while working.

'Painting the roses red'

Roses – some are white, some are red and some are a mixture.

The Gardeners – worked as the playing-cards but with black hoods and limbs.

Diag. 55 *'Painting the roses red'*

Diag. 56 *The White Rabbit*

Diag. 57 *The Caterpillar*

Fig. 42 *'The White Rabbit blew three blasts on the trumpet'*

The White Rabbit

The Banner – worked as a King of Hearts playing-card. Each coloured piece is outlined and filled in with the correct colour making sure that each piece joins to the next. Some areas are embroidered to form the red hearts and the blue-dotted collar.

The Caterpillar

The toadstool – the lines radiate on the under side and are worked by the triangular wedge method (p. 53). The spots are white couronnes, worked separately and attached afterwards.

Fig. 43 *'The caterpillar was sitting on top of the mushroom with its arms folded, quietly smoking a hookah'*

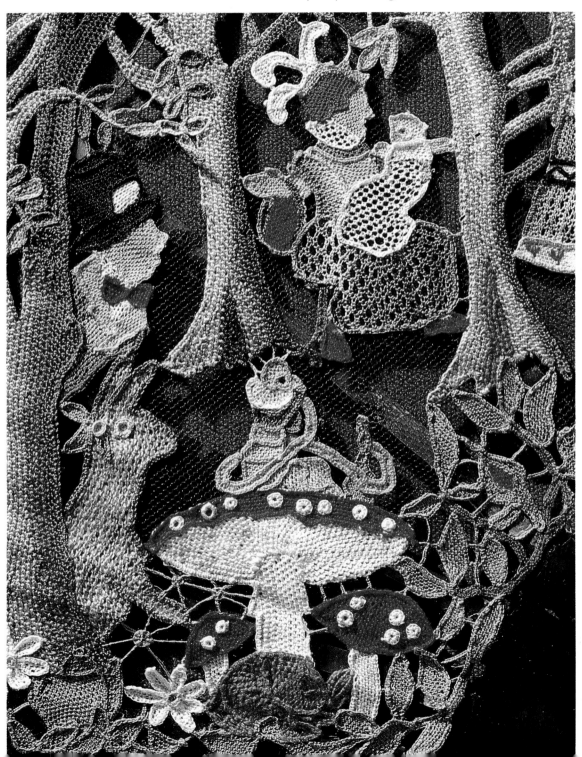

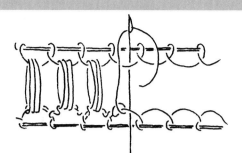

Diag. 58 *Beading*

FURTHER NEEDLELACE STITCHES

Beading
For filling a narrow space.

Work a row of Brussels stitch on either side of the area and join each loop with oversewn stitches – the loops lie side by side.

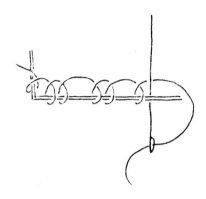

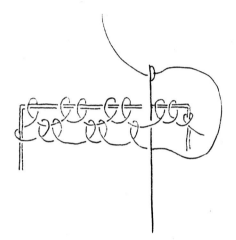

Double Brussels stitch
Work in the same way as for Brussels stitch but work the stitches in groups of two followed by a two-stitch space. This can be varied by the number of stitches in a group, threes, fours, etc. to form new fillings. (Combinations of 6–1–1–1–6 or 4–2–4–2, etc.)

Diags 59a & b *Double Brussels stitch*

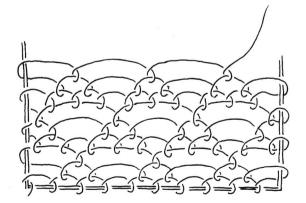

Diag. 60 *Pyramid stitch 1*

Pyramid stitches
Work in basic Brussels stitch.

Pyramid variation 1
Row 1 Work a row of Brussels stitch.
Row 2 Work two miss two.
Row 3 Work one miss three (over the same loop).
Row 4 Work three in every large loop.

Repeat the sequence.

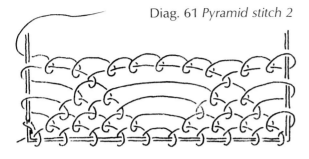

Diag. 61 *Pyramid stitch 2*

Pyramid variation 2

Row 1 Work a row of Brussels stitch.

Row 2 Work four miss two.

Row 3 Work three miss three.

Row 4 Work two miss four.

Row 5 Work one in the small loop and five in the large loop.

Repeat the sequence.

Point de Venise

With the needle towards you, make a single loop. Work three buttonhole stitches inside the loop and repeat across the row.

Turn and with the needle away from you, work Brussels stitch in each group of three in the previous row.

Turn and repeat the first row.

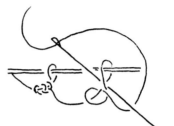

Diags 62a & b
Point de Venise

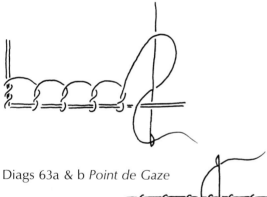

Diags 63a & b *Point de Gaze*

Alençon

This is a stitch with a twist worked from left to right. At the end of the first row, whip the thread through each loop back to the left side and repeat the row.

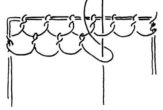

Point de Gaze

Work from left to right and turn the work as in Brussels stitch.

Form the buttonhole stitch by putting the thread from the needle under the needle, thus forming a twist (see Glossary).

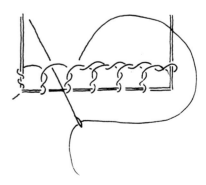

Diag. 64 *Point d'Alençon*

Fig. 44 *Hot-air balloons worked in needlelace with a bobbin lace background*

Fig. 45 *Brighton pavilion worked in needle- and bobbin lace to imitate a sepia photograph*

Fig. 46 *Mask fan in needle- and bobbin lace, made to use at a mediaeval banquet*

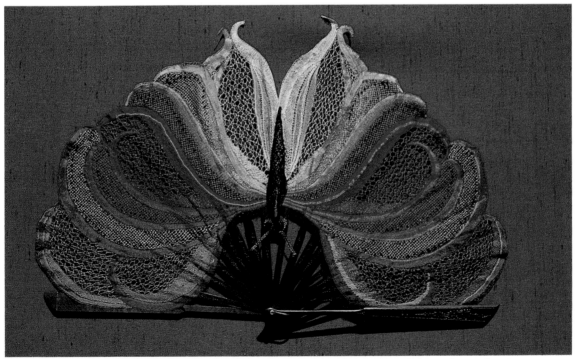

Fig. 47 *Butterfly fan in bobbin lace using the colours on the hot side of the colour wheel, worked in silk and metallic threads*

Glossary of terms

Alençon – whipped buttonhole stitch ground, used in Alençon lace

Appliqué – one piece of material applied to another with stitches to hold it firm

Architect's linen – blue, waxed-cotton fabric used by architects

Buttonhole stitch – commonly used to describe the stitch for needlelace

Circular graph paper – polar graph paper for producing a curved grid

Cordonnet – term used in Britain for the outlining thread in needlelace, but used on the Continent to mean the top stitching. (See *Fil de Trace* below)

Cordonette – a term used only in Britain (but not in this book) to mean the final top stitching, worked over the cordonnet

Couching – when a thread or threads are held in place by another oversewing them

Couching thread – fine thread used to couch down a laid thread.

Couronnes – buttonhole rings worked separately and attached to needlelace

Fil de trace – continental term for the outlining thread

Fillings – term used to describe the fancy stitches used in all laces

Gimp – thread used to outline some bobbin laces

– laid between the twists of the ground

Ground – term used to describe the background net of bobbin and needlelace

Limited palette – use of very few colours

Ne – open material, usually with hexagonal holes, machine made in cotton, silk or nylon. Sometimes used to describe the open work ground of bobbin lace

Outlining – laid couched thread which is the foundation for all needlelace (See *Fil de Trace*)

Passives – bobbin threads which lie as warp threads in a woven area

Picots – small excrescences

added to bars and edges in needlelace. Also used to describe the looped edge in Carrickmacross

Pillow – firmly packed straw cushion used for bobbin lace; a smaller version is sometimes used for needlelace

Point – term meaning a needle stitch

Point de Gaze – type of nineteenth-century, Belgian needlelace or the stitch used in the making of it

Point de Venise – Venetian needlelace stitch

Ring stick – graduated wooden stick for making couronnes

Spider Wheel – woven or buttonhole stitched central

hub with radiating struts

Tally – bobbin lace woven block made with 2 prs bobbins

Top stitching – final buttonhole stitching over two or more threads used to finish the edges of needlelace (See *Cordonnet*)

Torchon – one-piece geometric bobbin lace

Weavers – pair of threads used in bobbin lace for weaving a cloth stitch area

Whipping – oversewing or overcasting

Worked bars – two or three threads laid across a space and loop stitched or buttonholed

Books referred to in the text

BATSFORD, *Anchor Manual of Needlework*, B.T. Batsford, 1958

BIRREN, F., *Principles of Colour*, Van Nostrand Reinold, 1977

CARROLL, L., *Alice in Wonderland* (Illustrated by M. W. Tarrent), Ward Lock Sunshine Series

DE DILLMONT, T., *Encyclopaedia of Needlework*, DMC

KORTELAHTI, E-L., *Bobbin lace*, Kortelahti, 1988

THOMAS, M., *Dictionary of embroidery stitches*, Hodder & Stoughton, 1934

Further reading

Inspiration

ADDETTA, J., *Treasury of Chinese motifs*, Dover

GILLON, E. V., *Art Nouveau, An Anthology of Design from 'The Studio'*, Dover

GOS, F. & BALDOUSKI, K., *Alpine flower design for artists and craftsmen*, Dover, 1980

GRAFTON, C. B., *300 Art Nouveau designs*, Dover

HAECKEL, E., *Art forms in nature*, Dover, 1974

HARLOW, W. M., *Art forms in plant life*, Dover, 1976

McDOWELL, P., *Pressed flower collages*, Lutterworth Press, 1971

MENTON, T., *Chinese paper cuts*, Dover

MESSENT, J., *Embroidery and animals*, Batsford, 1984

MESSENT, J., *Embroidery and nature*, Batsford, 1980

MILLER, J., *House of Tours II* (stained glass) Miller. J.

MIROW, G., *Treasury of design for artists and craftsmen*, Dover, 1969

NICHOLS, M., *Designs and patterns for embroiderers and craftsmen*, Dover, 1974

SIBBETT, E. (Jr), *Floral stained glass pattern book*, Dover

VOYSEY, C., *Needle lace in photographs*, Batsford, 1987

Techniques

DILLMONT, T. DE, *Encyclopedia of needlework*, DMC

GIBSON, P. & HILLS, R., *Needle lace stitches*, Dryad Press, 1989

GROVES, E., *A new approach to embroidered net*, Dryad Press, 1987

HOLMES, D., *Flowers in needlepoint lace*, Dryad Press, 1987

KORTELAHTI, E-L., *Bobbin lace*, Kortelahti, 1988

NOTTINGHAM, P., *Torchon lace*, Batsford, 1979

SNOOK, B., *Embroidery stitches*, Dryad Press, 1963

STEVENS, A. & RICHARDSON, I., *Starting Zele lace*, Dryad Press, 1989

STILLWELL, , A., *Drafting Torchon lace patterns*, Dryad Press, 1986

THOMAS, M., *Dictionary of embroidery stitches*, Hodder & Stoughton, 1934

Suppliers and sources of information

General Suppliers:

United Kingdom

Alby Lace Museum
Cromer Road
Alby
Norfolk
NR11 7QE

Busy Bobbins
Unit 7
Scarrots Lane
Newport
Isle of Wight
PO30 1JD

Chosen Crafts Centre
46 Winchcombe Street
Cheltenham
Gloucestershire
GL52 2ND

Jo Firth
Lace Marketing &
Needlecraft Supplies
58 Kent Crescent
Lowton
Pudsey
West Yorkshire
LS28 9EB

J. & J. Ford
October Hill
Upper Way
Upper Longdon
Rugeley
Staffordshire
WS15 1QB

Framecraft
83 Hampstead Road
Handsworth Wood
Birmingham
B2 1JA

Doreen Gill
14 Barnfield Road
Petersfield
Hampshire
GU31 4DQ

R. Gravestock
Highwood
Crews Hill
Alfrick
Worcestershire
WR6 5HF

The Handicraft Shop
47 Northgate
Canterbury
Kent
CT1 1BE

Frank Herring & Sons
27 High West Street
Dorchester
Dorset
DT1 1UP

Honiton Lace Shop
44 High Street
Honiton
Devon

D. J. Hornsby
149 High Street
Burton Latimer
Kettering
Northamptonshire
NN15 5RL
also at:
25 Manwood Avenue
Canterbury
Kent
CT2 7AH

Frances Iles
73 High Street
Rochester
Kent
ME1 1LX

Jane's Pincushions
Unit 4
Taverham Crafts
Taverham Nursery Centre
Fir Covent Road
Taverham
Norwich
NR8 6HT

Loricraft
19 Peregrine Way
Grove
Wantage
Oxfordshire

Needlestyle
5 The Woolmead
Farnham
Surrey
GU9 7TX

Needlestyle
24–26 West Street
Alresford
Hampshire

Needlework
Ann Bartlee
Bucklers Farm
Coggeshall
Essex
CO6 1SB

Needle and Thread
80 High Street
Horsell
Woking
Surrey
GU21 4SZ

The Needlewoman
21 Needless Alley
off New Street
Birmingham
B2 5AE

T. Parker
124 Corhampton Road
Boscombe East
Bournemouth
Dorset
BH6 5NZ

Jane Playford
North Lodge
Church Close
West Runton
Norfolk
NR27 9QY

Redburn Crafts
Squires Garden Centre
Halliford Road
Upper Halliford
Shepperton
Middlesex
TW17 8RU

Christine Riley
53 Barclay Street
Stonehaven
Kincardineshire
Scotland

Peter & Beverley Scarlett
Strupak
Hill Head
Cold Wells
Ellon
Grampian
Scotland

Ken & Pat Schultz
134 Wisbech Road
Thornley
Peterborough

J. S. Sear
Lacecraft Supplies
8 Hill View
Sherrington
Buckinghamshire
MK16 9NY

Seblace
Waterloo Mills
Howden Road
Silsden
West Yorkshire
RD2 0NA

A. Sells
49 Pedley Lane
Clifton
Shefford
Bedfordshire

Shireburn Lace
Finkle Court
Finkle Hill
Sherburn in Elmet
North Yorkshire
LS25 6EB

SMP
4 Garners Close
Chalfont St Peter
Buckinghamshire
SL9 0HB

Southern Handicrafts
20 Kensington Gardens
Brighton
Sussex
BN1 4AC

Spangles
Carole Morris
Burwell
Cambridgeshire
CB5 0ED

Stitches
Dovehouse Shopping Parade
Warwick Road
Olton
Solihull
West Midlands

Teazle Embroideries
35 Boothferry Road
Hull
North Humberside

Valley House Crafts Studios
Ruston
Scarborough
North Yorkshire

George Walker
The Corner Shop
Rickinghall
Diss
Norfolk

West End Lace Supplies
Ravensworth Court Road
Mortimer West End
Reading
Berkshire
RG7 3UD

George White Lacemakers'
Supplies
40 Heath Drive
Boston Spa
West Yorkshire
L23 6PB

Bobbins

A. R. Arches
The Poplars
Shetland
near Stowmarket
Suffolk
IP14 3DE

T. Brown
Temple Lane Cottage
Littledean
Cinderford
Gloucestershire

Chrisken Bobbins
26 Cedar Drive
Kingsclere
Buckinghamshire
RG15 8TD

Malcolm J. Fielding
2 Northern Terrace
Moss Lane
Silverdale
Lancashire
LA5 0ST

Richard Gravestock
Highwood
Crews Hill
Alfrick
Worcestershire
WR6 5HF

Larkfield Crafts
Hilary Rickitts
4 Island Cottages
Mapledurwell
Basingstoke
Hampshire
RG25 2LU

Loricraft
19 Peregrine Way
Grove
Wantage
Oxfordshire

T. Parker
124 Corhampton Road
Boscombe East
Bournemouth
Dorset
BH6 5NZ

Bryan Phillips
Pantglas
Cellan
Lampeter
Dyfed
SA48 8JD

D. H. Shaw
47 Lamor Crescent
Thrushcroft
Rotherham
South Yorkshire
S66 9QD

Sizelands
1 Highfield Road
Winslow
Buckinghamshire
MK10 3QU

Christine & David Springett
21 Hillmorton Road
Rugby
Warwickshire
CV22 5DF

Richard Viney
Unit 7
Port Royal Street
Southsea
Hampshire
PO5 3UD

West End Lace Suppliers
Ravensworth Court Road
Mortimer West End
Reading
Berkshire
RG7 3UD

Gemstones and Jewellery findings

Gaycharm Ltd (mail order)
168 Chadwell Heath Road
Romford
Essex
RM6 6HT

Gold threads and fine wire

Stephen Simpson (mail order)
Avenham Road Works
Preston
Lancashire

Lace pillows

Newnham Lace Equipment
15 Marlowe Close
Basingstoke
Hampshire
RG24 9DD

Nets

Romance Bridals (mail order)
12 D'Arblay Street
London
W1

Books

Christopher Williams
19 Morrison Avenue
Parkstone
Poole
Dorset
BH17 4AD

Silk embroidery and lace thread

E. & J. Piper
Silverlea
Flax Lane
Glemsford
Suffolk
CO10 7RS

Silk weaving yarn

Hilary Chetwynd
Kipping Cottage
Cheriton
Alresford
Hampshire
SO24 0PW

Frames and mounts

Doreen Campbell
Highcliff
Brenisham Road
Malmesbury
Wiltshire

Matt coloured transparent adhesive film

Heffers Graphic Shop
26 King Street
Cambridge
CB1 1LN

Linen by the metre (yard) and made up articles of church linen

Mary Collins
Church Furnishings
St Andrews Hall
Humber Doucy Lane
Ipswich
Suffolk
IP4 3BP

Hayes & Finch
Head Office & Factory
Hanson Road
Aintree
Liverpool
L9 9BP

General suppliers overseas

United States of America

Arbor House
22 Arbor Lane
Rosyln Hights
NY 11577

Baltazor Inc.
3262 Severn Avenue
Metairie
LA 7002

Beggars' Lace
P.O. Box 17263
Denver
Colorado 80217

Berga Ullman Inc.
P.O. Box 918
North Adams
Massachusetts 01247

Frederick J. Fawcett
129 South Street
Boston
Massachusetts 02130

Frivolité
15526 Densmore N.
Seattle
Washington 98113

Happy Hands
3007 S. W. Marshall
Pendleton
Oregon 97180

International Old Lacers
P.O. Box 1029
Westminster
Colorado 80030

Lace Place de Belgique
800 S. W. 17th Street
Boca Raton
FL 33432

Lacis
2150 Stuart Street
Berkeley
California 9470

Robin's Bobbins
RTL Box 1736
Mineral Bluff
Georgia 30559

Robin and Russ
Handweavers
533 North Adams Street
McMinnvills
Oregon 97128

Some Place
2990 Adline Street
Berkeley
California 94703

Osma G. Todd Studio
319 Mendoza Avenue
Coral Gables
Florida 33134

The Unique And Art Lace
Cleaners
5926 Delman Boulevard
St Louis
Missouri 63112

Van Scriver Bobbin Lace
130 Cascadilla Park
Ithaca
New York 14850

The World in Stitches
82 South Street
Milford
N.H. 03055

Australia

Dentelles Lace Supplies
3 Narrak Close
Jindalee
Queensland 4074

The Lacemaker
94 Fordham Avenue
Hartwell
Victoria 3124

Spindle and Loom
Arcade 83
Longueville Road
Lane Cove
NSW 2066

Tulis Crafts
201 Avoca Street
Randwick
NSW 2031

Belgium

't Handwekhuisje
Katelijnestraat 23
8000 Bruges

Kantcentrum
Balstraat 14
8000 Bruges

Manufacture Belge de
Dentelle
6 Galerie de la Reine
Galeries Royales St Hubert
1000 Bruxelles

Orchidee
Mariastraat 18
8000 Bruges

Ann Thys
't Apostelientje
Balstraat 11
8000 Bruges

France

Centre d'Initiations à la
Dentelle du Puy
2 Rue Duguesclin
43000 Le Puy en Velay

A L'Econome
Anne-Marie Deydier
Ecole de Dentelle aux
Fuseaux
10 rue Paul Chenavard
69001 Lyon

Rougier and Ple
13–15 bd des Filles de
Calvaire
75003 Paris

West Germany

Der Fenster Laden
Berliner Str. 8
D 6483 Bad Soden
Salmunster

P.P. Hempel
Ortolanweg 34
1000 Berlin 47

Heikona De Ruijter
Kleoppelgrosshandel
Langer Steinweg 38
D4933 Blomberg

Holland

Blokker's Boektiek
Bronsteeweg 4/4a
2101 AC Heemstede

Theo Brejaat
Postbus 5199
3008 AD Rotterdam

Magazijn *De Vlijt*
Lijnmarkt 48
Utrecht

Switzerland

Fadehax
Inh. Irene Solca
4105 Biel-Benken
Basel

New Zealand

Peter McLeavey
P.O. Box 69.007
Auckland 8

Sources of Information

The Lace Guild
The Hollies
53 Audnam
Stourbridge
West Midlands
DY8 4AE

The Lacemakers' Circle
49 Wardwick
Derby
DE1 1HY

The Lace Society
Linwood
Stratford Road
Oversley
Alcester
Warwickshire
BY9 6PG

The British College of Lace
21 Hillmorton Road
Rugby
Warwickshire
CV22 5DF

The English Lace School
Oak House
Church Stile
Woodbury
Nr Exeter
Devon

International Old Lacers
President
Gunvor Jorgensen
366 Bradley Avenue
Northvale
NJ 076647
United States

United Kingdom Director
of International Old Lacers
S. Hurst
4 Dollius Road
London
N3 1RG

Ring of Tatters
Mrs C. Appleton
Nonesuch
5 Ryeland Road
Ellerby
Saltburn by Sea
Cleveland
TS13 5LP

Books

The following are stockists of the complete Batsford/Dryad Press range:

Avon

Bridge Bookshop
7 Bridge Street
Bath
BA2 4AS

Waterstone & Co.
4–5 Milsom Street
Bath
BA1 1DA

Bedfordshire

Arthur Sells
Lane Cove
49 Pedley Lane
Clifton
Sefford
SG17 5QT

Berkshire

West End Lace Supplies
Ravensworth Court Road
Mortimer West End
Reading
RG7 3UD

Buckinghamshire

J. S. Sear Lacecraft Supplies
8 Hill View
Sherringham
MK16 9NY

Cambridgeshire

Dillons The Bookstore
Sydney Street
Cambridge

Cheshire

Lyn Turner
Church Meadow Crafts
15 Carisbrook Drive
Winsford

Devon

Creative Crafts &
Needlework
18 High Street
Totnes
TQ9 5NP

Honiton Lace Shop
44 High Street
Honiton
EX14 8PJ

Dorset

F. Herring & Sons
High West Street
Dorchester
DT1 1UP

Tim Parker (mail order)
124 Corhampton Road
Boscombe East
Bournemouth
BH6 5NL

Durham

Lacemaid
6, 10 & 15 Stoneybeck
Bishop Middleham
DL17 9BL

Gloucestershire

Southgate Handicrafts
63 Southgate Street
Gloucester
GL1 1TX

Waterstone & Co.
89–90 The Promenade
Cheltenham
GL50 1NB

Hampshire

Creative Crafts
11 The Square
Winchester
SO23 9ES

Doreen Gill
14 Barnfield Road
Petersfield
GU31 4DR

Larkfield Crafts
4 Island Cottages
Mapledurwell
Basingstoke
RG23 2LU

Needlestyle
24–26 West Street
Alresford

Ruskins
27 Bell Street
Romsey

Isle of Wight

Busy Bobbins
Unit 7
Scarrots Lane
Newport
PO30 1JD

Kent

The Handicraft Shop
47 Northgate
Canterbury

Frances Iles
73 High Street
Rochester
ME1 1LX

Lincolnshire

Rippingale Lace
Barn Farm House
off Station Road
Rippingdale Bourne

London

Foyles
119 Charing Cross Road
WC2H 0EB

Hatchards
187 Piccadilly
W1

Middlesex

Redburn Crafts
Squires Garden Centre
Halliford Road
Upper Halliford
Shepperton
TW17 8RU

Norfolk

Alby Lace Museum
Cromer Road
Alby
Norwich
NR11 7QE

Jane's Pincushions
Taverham Craft Unit 4
Taverham Nursery Centre
Fir Covert Road
Taverham
Norwich
NR8 6HT

Waterstone & Co.
30 London Street
Norwich
NR2 1LD

Northamptonshire

D. J. Hornsby
149 High Street
Burton Latimer
Kettering
NN15 5RL

Oxfordshire

Loricraft
19 Peregrine Way
Grove
Wantage

Scotland

Embroidery Shop
51 Withain Street
Edinburgh
Lothian
EH3 7LW

Beverley Scarlett
Strupak
Hillhead
Coldwells
Ellon
Aberdeenshire

Waterstone & Co.
236 Union Street
Aberdeen
AB1 1TN

Surrey

Needlestyle
5 The Woolmead
Farnham
GU9 1TN

Sussex

Southern Handicrafts
20 Kensington Gardens
Brighton
BN1 4AL

Warwickshire

Christine & David Springett
21 Hillmorton Road
Rugby
CV22 6DF

North Yorkshire

Shireburn Lace
Finkel Court
Finkel Hill
Sherburn in Elmet
N. Yorks
LS25 6EA

Valley House Craft Studios
Ruston
Scarborough

West Midlands

Needlewoman
Needles Alley
off New Street
Birmingham

West Yorkshire

Seblace
Waterloo Mill
Howden Road
Silsden
BD20 0HA

George White Lacemaking
Supplies
40 Heath Drive
Boston Spa
LS23 6PB

Jo Firth
58 Kent Crescent
Lowtown
Pudsey
Leeds LS28 9EB

Index